BLISS BITES

BLISS BITES

kate bradley

Hardie Grant

BOOKS

CONTENTS

INTRODUCTION

From the very beginning of my journey into plant-based eating, it was a challenge to find tasty recipes that met my allergy and dietary requirements head on. Bliss bites have been one of my best discoveries; they're so fail-safe and now I find myself making them regularly. They were a revelation to me and I like to think of them as a 'healthy' truffle – easy to make and filled with great, nutritious ingredients.

Bliss bites have been a godsend on the cooking front too as there isn't much that can go wrong when you make them. This wasn't the case when I first started making plant-based alternatives to all my favourite foods. As in... "I know, I'll make a healthy chocolate cake with no refined sugar, gluten, dairy, eggs, fat or nuts in it. What could possibly go wrong?" *Absolutely everything.*

In the early days of my plant-based cooking, half my experiments ended up resembling inedible pieces of (expensive) cardboard, or some sort of crumbly disaster. Lucky for me I have a boyfriend who wouldn't let even the worst of my experiments go to waste. Thanks, Bulut!

But when it came to making bliss bites, there were never any issues of failure. It seemed that I could just throw any combination of ingredients into my food processor, then out would come some delicious mixture that could be rolled into bite-sized bites and eaten. So, so simple. I tell you, these things are pure genius.

After a few experiments, bliss bites of every conceivable variety began to make their way into my weekly food prep routine. I loved the fact I could make big batches of them, each with their own health purpose and benefits, then refrigerate or freeze them for whenever the bliss-ball urge struck. I could take them to university as a great energy-boosting, in-between-class snack for myself (and a during-class-snack, to avoid falling asleep). I could feed them to my sport-mad brother to ensure he was getting plenty of protein in his diet, and give them to my mum, who has a habit of forgetting to eat during the day. This is a problem I've certainly never had – actually, it's more the opposite case for me.

Something else I really love about bliss bites is that everyone and anyone can make them. You don't need to be an experienced cook as there's nothing technical about the process at all. If you can measure ingredients, press the button on a food processor or blender and use your hands to roll small amounts of a mixture into balls, you're there.

When I first started eating plant-based foods, I was quite intimidated by many of the recipes I found. They were complex, filled with ingredients I couldn't pronounce and that I had no idea about sourcing. The recipes seemed totally unrealistic to make due to their ingredient cost – especially on a student's budget. Although it's six years since my initial move to plant-based eating, and the hard-to-find, unpronounceable ingredients are thankfully more accessible now, it's still easy to be overwhelmed by some of the recipes you encounter.

As I don't think anyone should be intimidated by food, this cookbook has been designed differently. It's not just for those who can afford fancy 'superfood' powders and mystical oils and herbs. Whilst these are nice, they aren't a reality for everyone. Instead, this book has been designed for anyone who just wants to create healthy snack alternatives with ease. Therefore all the ingredients I use are readily available from the health section of the supermarket or your local health food shop.

Don't get me wrong, you don't have to make these at home. You can buy bliss bites everywhere now. They are on supermarket shelves, sold at gyms, cafes and, of course, at health food shops. Store-buying can be an easy and quick solution, but paying $4–$5 per tiny ball can be depressing. Not to mention destructive to your bank balance. They do tend to be pricey. Plus, those commercially available balls are not always as healthy as they could be. Making home-made balls will not only save you money, but you'll end up making something healthier and I guarantee, you'll win plenty of love from friends and family in the process.

Before you freak out at possible bliss bite overkill, rest assured there are more than just balls in this cookbook. Creating 60-plus ball recipes, all of them sweet, would have been madness, and I probably would have had some sort of nervous, ball-related breakdown in the process. So I also created an array of other bite-sized goodies; you'll find savouries and drinks here, as well as other sweets, such as Breakfast bars and healthy alternatives of classic chocolate bars, including Bounty bars and Snickers bars. Every recipe in this book is perfect for snacking, to include in your lunch and for general, on-the-go consumption. Of course I did have to include some classic treats, reimagined in a 'healthier' way as a bliss bite... did someone say TWIX?

Above all, the recipes in this book are designed to be easy. My goal with them is not to scare you, or have you think that making a delicious, healthy snack is a tricky task. It's *so* not. Literally within minutes, you can have something delicious whipped up, whether to take to work during the week, serve instead of a dessert, or just to have on hand for a bit of spontaneous indulgence.

I've tried to cater for as many allergies, intolerances and dietary preferences as I can, so if you're vegan, gluten-free or dairy-free, you'll find options here that will work for you. Some of these recipes are nut-free too.

There isn't a single person I know who doesn't love a tasty bliss bite or two, and I hope that you will love them too.

Kate xx

YOUR BLISS BITE STARTER KIT

So you want to be a bliss baller? Consider this your extended starter pack – from the must-haves, to the nice-to-haves, to the luxury items. With these, you'll be able to make delicious balls and snacks whenever you please. Of course, you don't need to buy every ingredient here, and you don't need to fill your pantry all at once either. But having a good mix of some of the following will make it a lot easier when you want to get ballin' and don't want to make a special shopping excursion to do so.

STARTER PACK ESSENTIALS

- a variety of nuts (e.g. almonds, cashews, walnuts, macadamias and peanuts)
- nut and seed butters (e.g. sesame, almond and coconut)
- flax seeds (linseeds)
- sunflower seeds
- chia seeds
- pepitas (pumpkin seeds)
- sesame seeds (black and white)
- linseed (flax seed) meal
- medjool dates
- desiccated coconut
- shredded coconut
- ground almonds
- arrowroot/tapioca flour
- quinoa
- sushi rice
- arborio rice
- millet
- gluten-free oats
- oils (grapeseed and coconut)
- sweeteners (maple syrup, rice malt syrup and raw honey)
- coconut cream
- coconut milk
- coconut water
- nut and seed milks (e.g. almond, cashew, hemp and sesame)
- cider vinegar
- tamari
- sparkling water
- tinned beans (e.g. chickpeas, black beans, cannellini [lima] beans)
- frozen berries
- ground spices (e.g. turmeric, nutmeg, cinnamon and ginger)
- raw chocolate
- cacao powder
- nutritional yeast
- gluten-free breadcrumbs
- spirulina/super greens powder
- salt flakes
- baking powder
- baking soda

NICE TO HAVE

- dried fruits (e.g. blueberries, apricots, mango, peach and strawberries)
- goji berries
- coconut flakes
- beetroot (beet) powder
- rolled buckwheat
- quinoa flakes
- puffed quinoa
- brown rice puffs
- kimchi
- dukkah
- za'atar
- cacao nibs
- psyllium husks
- wakame and kelp
- carob powder
- miso paste
- matcha powder
- vanilla powder
- natural vanilla extract
- acai powder
- maca powder
- plant-based protein powder (e.g. vanilla, chocolate, berry or unflavoured)
- maple syrup
- hemp seeds
- coconut flour
- coconut sugar
- buckwheat flour
- tinned artichokes
- cacao butter

ICING ON THE CAKE

- inca berries
- raspberry powder
- bee pollen
- caramelised buckwheat
- liquid smoke
- reishi powder
- chlorella powder
- camu camu powder
- cordyceps powder
- lucuma powder
- mesquite powder
- coconut nectar
- agave nectar
- LSA (linseed, sunflower seed and almond mix)
- rosewater
- orange blossom water

ACTIVATING INGREDIENTS

Activating ingredients, such as nuts, seeds and buckwheat groats, helps to break down chemical compounds that interfere with the absorption of nutrients. Activating also helps start the sprouting, or germination, process, which makes nuts and seeds easier to digest. You can buy ready-activated ingredients from most health food shops, but it's cheaper to make your own.

To activate your nuts or seeds, place 280 g (10 oz) nuts in a bowl and cover with water. Add 2 teaspoons salt to the water and mix well. Cover the bowl with a tea towel (dish towel) and leave to soak for 7–12 hours, or overnight. (Almonds may take longer – up to 14 hours – to soak.) Strain the nuts, then spread them out on a baking tray. Transfer to an oven preheated to the lowest possible temperature (usually between 50–65°C [120–150°F]) and leave to dry for 12–24 hours. Ensure the nuts are completely dry and crunchy before removing them from the oven as still-damp nuts can turn mouldy. Once completely cool, store your activated nuts and seeds in an airtight container in the refrigerator or in a sterilised jar (see below) at room temperature for up to 3 months.

STERILISING JARS

Glass jars used for storing and preserving need to be sterilised before use to avoid contamination. To sterilise jars, remove the lids and wash the jars thoroughly in warm soapy water. Place jars, mouths up, on a baking tray and place in a low oven until completely dried. The lids should be boiled for 10 minutes and left to air-dry on a clean tea towel (dish towel).

USING THIS BOOK AS A GUIDE

These recipes have been rigorously tested and are good to go as they are. However, they have also been developed with flexibility in mind, so you can freely play around with them to suit your own tastes and needs. Ingredients can be substituted where required (e.g. to suit an allergy or to fit with what's in your pantry). Use these recipes as guides only and find combinations of ingredients for them that work best for you.

MAKING THE RECIPES NUT-FREE

Not all recipes in this book can be made nut-free but, where possible, I have included the option to create a nut-free bite or snack. There are a few ways to make recipes nut-free; the simplest is by substituting nutty ingredients with a seed alternative.

For example, where almond meal is listed, sunflower meal can be used instead. To make sunflower meal, place raw, activated or toasted sunflower seeds in your food processor or high-speed blender and pulse them until a fine meal forms. Avoid over-processing, or you will end up with sunflower seed butter.

Where a nut butter is listed, sunflower or pepita (pumpkin seed) butter can be used.

BASIC SUNFLOWER SEED BUTTER

MAKES 375 G (13 OZ 1½ CUPS)
Preparation time: 15 minutes

---

375 g (13 oz/3 cups) raw or toasted
  sunflower seeds (see note)

maple syrup, to taste
pinch salt

Place all the ingredients into your food processor or blender and process until smooth. Transfer into a sterilised jar (see page 11) and store in the fridge.

NOTE
For a nuttier tasting butter, use roasted sunflower seeds. Heat the oven to 180°C (350°F), spread the seeds thinly over a large baking tray and roast for 15–20 minutes or until they are light golden. Let them cool before blending.

STORAGE

Recipes in this book are best stored in an airtight container in the fridge or freezer. Recipes using fresh and/or raw ingredients are best kept in the freezer if they will not be consumed within the first few days of making.

Nº 1

EVERYDAY STAPLES

SUPERFOOD SUPER-GOOD BLISS BALLS

MAKES 30
Preparation time: 20 minutes

These are the perfect, tasty snack to pop into kids' lunchboxes. Or, into your
own bag to nibble on while you're on the run and trying not to be tempted by junk food.
Throw some optional protein powder into these too if you like, and use them as a little
post-workout treat. Delicious flavour bites at any time; just the thought of eating these
makes me feel great.

60 g (2 oz/½ cup) sunflower seeds
70 g (2½ oz/½ cup) pepitas (pumpkin seeds)
40 g (1½ oz/¼ cup) black or white chia
   seeds
30 g (1 oz/½ cup) shredded coconut
40 g (1½ oz/¼ cup) brazil nuts
40 g (1½ oz/¼ cup) almonds
30 g (1 oz/¼ cup) hemp seeds

2½ tablespoons bee pollen (optional)
1 tablespoon ground cinnamon
40 g (1½ oz/⅓ cup) raw cacao powder
40 g (1½ oz/⅓ cup) plant-based protein
   powder (see note, optional)
14 medjool dates (about 280g/10 oz),
   pitted
80 ml (2½ fl oz/⅓ cup) rice malt syrup
desiccated coconut, for rolling

Place the sunflower seeds, pepitas, chia seeds and shredded coconut in your food
processor or blender and pulse until a fine meal is formed. Add the brazil nuts and
almonds and pulse until they are finely chopped but still have a bit of texture; they
shouldn't be like meal (see note).

Transfer the mixture to a bowl and add the hemp seeds, bee pollen (if using),
cinnamon, raw cacao powder and protein powder (if using).

Place the dates and rice malt syrup in the food processor or blender and process
until smooth. Add to the dry ingredients in the bowl and combine well – you may
need to get your hands in there and really mush the ingredients together if mixing it
with a spoon isn't doing the trick. (Just make sure you wash those hands first!) Add
a tablespoon of water if the mixture seems a bit dry.

Next, take about a tablespoon of the mixture at a time and roll it into 2.5 cm
(1 in) balls. Roll the balls in the desiccated coconut to lightly coat then place them in
an airtight container. Refrigerate or freeze them. These will keep for up to 2 weeks
in the fridge, and a couple of months in the freezer.

NOTE
If you want a softer truffle, pulse the ingredients until everything is a fine meal. Use any
flavour protein powder you like – chocolate, vanilla or coconut, for example.

BERRY PROTEIN BOMBS

MAKES 16
Preparation time: 10 minutes

Oh man, my family (and friends who have tried them) LOVE these. These are not only super simple to make, they're flavour-packed, protein-packed and antioxidant-packed! The combination of different berries is killer and the protein powder makes the consistency fudgy and awesome. If you want, you can substitute goji berries for one of the types of berry in this recipe. I like to leave these in the fridge for a snack to have either before or after a workout. Or, for when I want something sweet, but don't want to feel gross afterwards.

50 g (1¾ oz/½ cup) berry flavoured plant-based protein powder
1 teaspoon acai powder
90 g (3 oz/⅓ cup) almond or seed butter
40 ml (1¼ fl oz) maple syrup
1 tablespoon raw honey or rice malt syrup
55 g (2 oz/½ cup) ground almonds

1 teaspoon vanilla extract or ½ teaspoon vanilla powder
3 medjool dates (about 60 g/2 oz), pitted
50 g (1¾ oz/⅓ cup) dried blueberries
50 g (1¾ oz/⅓ cup) dried strawberries
50 g (1¾ oz/⅓ cup) dried raspberries

Place the protein powder, acai powder, almond butter, maple syrup, honey, ground almonds, vanilla and dates in your food processor or blender and pulse until smooth. Throw in the dried berries and pulse until they are just crushed.

Take about a tablespoon of the mixture at a time and roll it into 3.5 cm (1½ in) balls. Place them in an airtight container then refrigerate or freeze them. These will keep for up to 2 weeks in the fridge, and a couple of months in the freezer.

5-INGREDIENT PEANUT BUTTER BLISS BALLS

MAKES 12
Preparation time: 10 minutes

For those with a peanut butter weakness-slash-obsession, like me (high-five, fellow obsessives!), these bliss balls will be your go-to. They are simple and convenient to make, needing no food processor or blender, and requiring only five ingredients.

125 g (4½ oz/½ cup) crunchy peanut butter
90 g (3 oz/1 cup) desiccated coconut
2½ tablespoons raw cacao powder

40 ml (1¼ fl oz) maple syrup
pinch sea salt flakes

Combine all the ingredients in a mixing bowl then stir until combined.

Take about a tablespoon of mixture at a time and roll it into 2.5 cm (1 in) balls. Place the balls in an airtight container in the fridge or freezer. These guys will keep for up to 2 weeks in the fridge, and a couple of months in the freezer. That's it. Told you they were easy.

I NEED A COFFEE BLISS BALLS

MAKES 16
Preparation time: 10 minutes

Sometimes, my morning coffee just isn't enough, no matter how many cups I have. These balls provide the perfect mid-morning kick to keep me going throughout the day and – bonus! – they're filled with healthy fats and are naturally sweetened. A few of these make a mighty fine stand-in for a regular afternoon coffee/biscuit combo.

2 tablespoons finely ground coffee
115 g (4 oz/¾ cup) raw or activated cashews (see page 11)
50 g (1¾ oz/½ cup) walnut halves
40 g (1½ oz) cashew butter
40 ml (1¼ fl oz) maple syrup

1 teaspoon vanilla extract or ½ teaspoon vanilla powder
5 medjool dates (about 100 g/3½ oz), pitted
75 g (2¾ oz/½ cup) golden or brown linseed (flax seed) meal
1½ tablespoons raw cacao powder, plus extra for rolling

Place all the ingredients in your food processor or blender and pulse until the mixture comes together to form a ball.

Take about a tablespoon of the mixture at a time and roll it into 2.5 cm (1 in) balls. Dust each ball in raw cacao powder then place them in an airtight container. These will keep for up to 2 weeks in the fridge, and a couple of months in the freezer.

GET YA GLOW ON BLISS BALLS

MAKES 30
Preparation time: 20 minutes

These balls are a variation of the original superfood balls (page 16) and will add brightness to any dull day! Not only do they look like balls of sunshine, but they are also packed with spices and seeds to help make you shine from the inside out! The bee pollen can be left out, or substituted with desiccated (shredded) coconut for rolling.

60 g (2 oz/½ cup) sunflower seeds
70 g (2½ oz/½ cup) pepitas (pumpkin seeds)
40 g (1½ oz/½ cup) white chia seeds
65 g (2¼ oz/⅔ cup) pecan nuts
30 g (1 oz/¼ cup) hemp seeds
2½ tablespoons bee pollen (optional)
1 tablespoon ground cinnamon
½ teaspoon ground turmeric

1 teaspoon maca powder
¼ teaspoon ground ginger
10 medjool dates (about 200 g/7 oz), pitted
70 g (2½ oz) dried figs
1 teaspoon vanilla extract
90 g (3 oz/¼ cup) raw honey or
  rice malt syrup
bee pollen or desiccated coconut, for rolling

Place the sunflower seeds, pepitas and chia seeds in your food processor or blender and pulse them together until a fine meal forms. Add the pecans and pulse just a few times or until they are broken up but still have plenty of texture (see note).

Transfer the mixture to a bowl and add the hemp seeds, bee pollen (if using), cinnamon, turmeric, maca powder and ginger.

In the clean food processor or blender, place the dates, figs, vanilla and honey then process until everything is smooth.

Add the date mixture to the bowl with the dry ingredients and use a wooden spoon to mix them together well. You may need to get your hands in there and really mush the ingredients together if mixing with a spoon is not doing the trick. (Just make sure you wash your hands first!) Add a tablespoon of water if the mixture seems too dry.

Take about a tablespoon of the mixture at a time and roll it into 2.5 cm (1 in) balls. Roll the balls in the bee pollen or desiccated coconut to lightly coat then place them in an airtight container and refrigerate or freeze them. These will keep for up to 2 weeks in the fridge, and a couple of months in the freezer.

NOTE
If you want a softer truffle, pulse the ingredients until everything is a fine meal.

CHOC MINT BLISS BALLS

MAKES 14
Preparation time: 10 minutes

———————

A simple, delicious and fresh-tasting snack to have while you're on the go, these little grain-free bites will keep your brain fuelled and those sweet cravings satisfied. Think of this no-guilt treat as a chocolate mint slice replacement, or if you're old-school, an after dinner mint replacement.

150 g (5½ oz/1½ cup) walnut halves
8 medjool dates (about 160 g/5½ oz), pitted
40 g (1½ oz) almond butter
30 g (1 oz/¼ cup) raw cacao powder

1 teaspoon vanilla extract or ½ teaspoon vanilla powder
3 drops peppermint essential oil, or 1 teaspoon peppermint essence, to taste

Place all the ingredients in your food processor or blender and pulse until combined well.

Take about a tablespoon of the mixture at a time and roll it into 2.5 cm (1 in) balls. Place the balls in an airtight container then refrigerate or freeze them. These will keep for up to 2 weeks in the fridge, and a couple of months in the freezer.

'JAFFA' CHOC-ORANGE BLISS BALLS

MAKES 14
Preparation time: 10 minutes

These choc-orange bliss balls are a Jaffa lover's delight. Try them as a great afternoon snack or as a mid-morning pick-me-up. They'll keep your day balanced and your sweet tooth satisfied. Add some chocolate protein powder (about 2 tablespoons) for some extra energy, or drizzle them with melted chocolate for a delicious dessert-time treat.

150 g (5½ oz/1½ cups) walnut halves
8 medjool dates (about 160 g/5½ oz), pitted
40 g (1½ oz) almond butter

30 g (1 oz/¼ cup) raw cacao powder
finely grated zest of 1 orange
3 drops orange essential oil, or 1 teaspoon orange essence, to taste

Place all the ingredients in your food processor or blender and pulse them together until combined.

Take about a tablespoon of the mixture at a time and roll it into 2.5 cm (1 in) balls. Place the balls in an airtight container in the fridge or freezer. These will keep for up to 2 weeks in the fridge, and a couple of months in the freezer.

EAT YOUR GREENS #1

(CHLORELLA & CACAO)

MAKES 15
Preparation time: 10 minutes

These are a great way to sneak those swampy algaes (spirulina and chlorella) into food.
I know there's nothing potentially more frightening than a bright, marshland-coloured
powder in food and drink, but this is a good way to get it in because you can't really
tell it's there. Super easy, these can also be made nut-free and cacao-free for kids'
lunchboxes, using the correct substitutions; use any seed butter (including tahini) you
like instead of the nut butter, carob instead of cacao and sunflower seed meal instead
of the ground almonds. WIN WIN!

155 g (5½ oz/1½ cups) ground almonds

2½ tablespoons coconut oil

2½ tablespoons ABC (almond, brazil and
cashew butter), or almond or cashew
nut butter

2½ tablespoons raw honey or maple syrup

1 teaspoon vanilla extract or ½ teaspoon
vanilla powder

8 medjool dates (about 160 g/5½ oz), pitted

1 tablespoon white or black chia seeds

40 g (1½ oz/⅓ cup) raw cacao powder or
carob powder

1 tablespoon chlorella or spirulina

1 teaspoon ground cinnamon

extra black chia seeds or hemp seeds
(see note), for rolling

Place all the ingredients in your food processor or blender and pulse them together
until combined.

Take about a tablespoon of the mixture at a time and roll it into 2.5 cm (1 in)
balls, then roll them in chia seeds to lightly coat. Place them in an airtight container
then refrigerate or freeze. These will keep for up to 2 weeks in the fridge, and a couple
of months in the freezer.

NOTE
Hemp seeds can be substituted for another seed and instead of the ground almonds,
you can use the same quantity of sunflower seeds ground to a meal in your food
processor.

(pictured on page 28)

EAT YOUR GREENS #2

(SUPERGREENS, HEMP & VANILLA PROTEIN)

MAKES 15
Preparation time: 10 minutes

This is a more hectic ball, I'm not going to lie. They are nut-free, date-free, cacao-free and they are, well, green. However, despite their colour and the more 'serious' ingredients they contain (greens powder is serious, after all), they are what I call Next Level Delicious. Some days you just don't want to eat kale (even though kale totally rules), and when that happens, you can feel good eating these instead.

125 g (4½ oz/1 cup) sunflower seeds
40 g (1½ oz/⅓ cup) hemp seeds, plus extra for rolling
2 tablespoons super greens powder
½ teaspoon matcha powder

45 g (1½ oz/½ cup) desiccated coconut
30 g (1 oz) vanilla flavoured plant-based protein powder
2½ tablespoons coconut oil
2½ tablespoons raw honey or maple syrup

Place the sunflower seeds, hemp seeds, greens powder, matcha powder, desiccated coconut, protein powder, coconut oil and honey in your food processor or blender and pulse until combined.

Take about a tablespoon of the mixture at a time and roll it into 2.5 cm (1 in) balls. Roll the balls in the extra hemp seeds to coat them lightly then place in an airtight container and refrigerate or freeze them. These will keep for up to 2 weeks in the fridge, and a couple of months in the freezer.

NOTE
Hemp seeds can be substituted for another seed, such as sesame seeds.

(pictured on page 29)

BLUEBERRY CRUNCH BLISS BALLS

MAKES 18
Preparation time: 10 minutes

Sometimes, you just need a bit of crunch and texture in your bliss balls, and these definitely have that. They're also a great replacement for the refined sugar-filled muesli bars you can get in bite form. Not only can these be whipped up in minutes, they will keep you energised to take on whatever the day throws at you.

80 g (2¾ oz/¾ cup) ground almonds

2 tablespoons coconut oil

40 g (1½ oz) ABC (almond, brazil and cashew butter), or almond or cashew butter

1 tablespoon raw honey or maple syrup

1 teaspoon vanilla extract or vanilla bean paste

5 medjool dates (about 100g/3½ oz), pitted

2½ tablespoons maca powder

80 g (2¾ oz) activated buckinis (see page 11)

50 g (1¾ oz/⅓ cup) pepitas (pumpkin seeds)

90 g (3 oz) dried blueberries

Place the ground almonds, coconut oil, nut butter, honey, vanilla, dates and maca powder in your food processor or blender and process until combined. Add the activated buckinis, the pepitas and blueberries and pulse once or twice until everything is combined but still has a bit of texture.

Take about a tablespoon of mixture at a time and roll it into 2.5 cm (1 in) balls. Place the balls in an airtight container and refrigerate or freeze. These will keep for up to 2 weeks in the fridge, and a couple of months in the freezer.

FRUIT SALAD BITES

MAKES 12
Preparation time: 15 minutes

A great lunchbox filler that will satisfy any cravings for sweetness, these bliss balls are a fruitier, nuttier, lighter option than most others. They're really flexible too. For example, you can add some grated lime zest if you want to get your tropical vibe on, and use different fruits, dried apple or pineapple, for example. On top of all this, they're super handy for those times when you want to brag that 'yeah, I've eaten like, five different fruits today'.

4–5 dried apricots (about 25 g/1 oz)
1 large dried mango cheek (about 30 g/1 oz)
5 dried peach halves (about 100 g/3½ oz)
4 dried pear halves (about 70 g/2½ oz)
90 g (3 oz/1 cup) desiccated coconut
55 g (2 oz/½ cup) ground almonds

30 g (1 oz/¼ cup) pepitas (pumpkin seeds) (optional)
2½ tablespoons raw honey or maple syrup
2½ tablespoons cashew butter
finely grated zest of 1 lime (optional)
½ teaspoon vanilla extract or ¼ teaspoon vanilla powder (optional)

Place all the ingredients in your food processor or blender and process them until combined.

Take about a tablespoon of the mixture at a time and roll it into 2.5 cm (1 in) balls. Place the balls in an airtight container and refrigerate or freeze. These will keep for up to 2 weeks in the fridge, and a couple of months in the freezer.

ACAI APPLE PIE BLISS BALLS

MAKES 14
Preparation time: 10 minutes

These are like an apple and berry pie, except in ball form. Not only does their colour look nice with the acai powder in there, but the acai also gives them a little antioxidant boost. And it's always good to have a bit of an antioxidant boost, I reckon.

150 g (5½ oz) walnut halves or sunflower seeds

7 medjool dates (about 140g/5 oz), pitted

40 g (1½ oz) cashew or seed butter

2 tablespoons acai powder

2 teaspoons beetroot (beet) powder (optional)

1 teaspoon ground cinnamon

200 g (7 oz/2⅔ cups) dried apple

1 teaspoon vanilla extract or ½ teaspoon vanilla powder

Place all the ingredients in your food processor or blender and pulse everything together until combined.

Take about a tablespoon of the mixture at a time and roll it into 2.5 cm (1 in) balls. Place the balls in an airtight container then refrigerate or freeze. These will keep for up to 2 weeks in the fridge, and a couple of months in the freezer.

CARROT CAKE BLISS BALLS

MAKES 12
Preparation time: 10 minutes

I love carrot cake, and clearly I love bliss balls. Combine these two concepts and you get carrot cake balls. Enough said.

150 g (5½ oz/1½ cups) walnut halves
10 medjool dates (about 200g/17 oz), pitted
1 large carrot, grated
1 teaspoon finely grated fresh ginger
½ teaspoon ground cinnamon
⅛ teaspoon freshly grated nutmeg
pinch sea salt flakes
50 g (1¾ oz) LSA (linseed, sunflower seed and almond mix) or ground almonds
finely grated zest of 1 lemon (optional)
70 g (2½ oz/1 cup) shredded coconut

Place all the ingredients, except the desiccated coconut, into your food processor or blender and process them until combined.

Take about a tablespoon of the mixture at a time and roll it into 2.5 cm (1 in) balls then roll the balls in the desiccated coconut to coat. Place the balls in an airtight container, then refrigerate or freeze them. These will keep for up to 2 weeks in the fridge, and a couple of months in the freezer.

NOTE

If you want some walnut chunks in here (which are so good), add an additional 30 g (1 oz/¼ cup) or so of crushed walnuts, after processing the mixture. Knock back the grated ginger to ½ teaspoon if you want a milder gingery-ness.

CHOCOLATE PROTEIN BOMBS

MAKES 16
Preparation time: 10 minutes

These chocolate protein balls are the perfect energy-fuelling snack to have before or after a workout. They are fudgy, chocolatey and totally delicious.

50 g (1¾ oz/½ cup) chocolate flavoured plant-based protein powder

1 tablespoon raw cacao powder

1 tablespoon maca powder

90 g (3 oz/⅓ cup) cashew butter (or any nut or seed butter)

90 g (3 oz/¼ cup) maple syrup, raw honey or rice malt syrup

55 g (2 oz/½ cup) ground almonds

1 teaspoon vanilla extract or ½ teaspoon vanilla powder

3 medjool dates (about 60 g/2 oz), pitted

35 g (1¼ oz/⅓ cup) goji berries

45 g (1½ oz/⅓ cup) inca berries (optional)

40 g (1½ oz/¼ cup) cacao nibs

Place the protein powder, raw cacao powder, maca powder, cashew butter, maple syrup, ground almonds, vanilla and dates in your food processor and pulse until a fine meal is formed. Add the goji and inca berries (if using) and pulse until they are just crushed.

Next, take about a tablespoon of mixture at a time and roll it into 2.5 cm (1 in) balls. Place them in an airtight container in the fridge or freezer. These will keep for up to 2 weeks in the fridge, and a couple of months in the freezer.

NOTE

To make these completely nut-free, replace the ground almonds with 60 g (2 oz/½ cup) sunflower seeds, blitzed into a meal in the food processor. And make sure you choose a seed butter instead of a nut butter.

LOVE BITES

MAKES 10
Preparation time: 10 minutes

These love bites not only look super loved-up (being pink), but they are also the perfect accompaniment for your next Netflix session. However, they're not intended for your platonic circle of friends, as they're filled with goodies that are intended to 'ignite the flame'. If you know what I mean.

90 g (3 oz/1 cup) desiccated coconut
100 g (3½ oz/1 cup) ground almonds
½ ripe banana
1 tablespoon white chia seeds
1 tablespoon beetroot (beet) powder
3 teaspoons ground cinnamon
1 tablespoon maca powder
2½ tablespoons pine nuts

2½ tablespoons raw honey, maple syrup or rice malt syrup
½ teaspoon ground cardamom
½ teaspoon vanilla powder
4 dried figs (about 90 g/3 oz)
finely grated zest of 1 orange (optional)
white chia seeds, bee pollen, desiccated coconut or raspberry powder, for rolling (optional)

Place all the ingredients except the chia seeds (or whatever else you're using to coat – if you are) into your food processor or blender. Process until everything is combined well and the mixture forms a ball.

Take about a tablespoon of the mixture at a time and roll it into 2.5 cm (1 in) balls. Roll the balls in the coating of your choice, if you like, then place them in an airtight container. Refrigerate or freeze them. These will keep for up to 5 days in the fridge, and a month in the freezer.

Nº 2

SAVOURY BITES

MEGA SEED CRACKERS

MAKES 15
Preparation time: 10 minutes
Drying time: 8 hours

I loooooove crackers. These ones are my ultimate snack. They're perfect for when you're travelling, for taking to work or just for when you're sprinting out the door and remember you haven't eaten anything yet. Spread them with some healthymite (see opposite), or just with coconut butter and raw honey (this is such an amazing combination). Either way, these are the best little snacks ever!

90 g (3 oz/½ cup) linseeds (flax seeds)
40 g (1½ oz/¼ cup) white or
   black chia seeds
40 g (1½ oz/¼ cup) sesame seeds
70 g (2½ oz) sunflower seeds

90 g (3 oz/⅔ cup) pepitas (pumpkin seeds)
2½ tablespoons psyllium husk
pinch sea salt flakes
310 ml (10½ fl oz/1¼ cups) water

Preheat the oven to 70°C (160°F) and line a baking tray with baking paper.

Combine all the ingredients in a mixing bowl and stir until combined well. Spread the mixture out evenly onto the baking tray, to form a 30 x 34 cm (11 x 13 in) rectangle, pressing it gently to pack it down slightly. Mark into 15 rough crackers about 10 x 7 cm (4 x 2¾ in). Place in the oven and leave to dehydrate for 8 hours or overnight. You can also pop these into a dehydrator. Once they're crunchy, remove them from the oven (or your dehydrator) and break them up into crackers. Place them in an airtight container and nibble as you please! Store in an airtight container for up to 1 month.

HEALTHYMITE

MAKES 250 G (9 OZ/½ CUP)
Preparation time: 5 minutes

When I first found out I was a coeliac sufferer, I was devastated. I could no longer
eat Vegemite, a savoury yeast spread that's a national obsession here in Australia.
I tried alternatives from the supermarket and they were well, gross, both in taste and
ingredients. This 'mite' is unlike any of the alternatives; it's totally Vegemitey, packed
with protein from the black tahini and still has those B vitamins I love in Vegemite.
These come from the nutritional yeast. This spread is a life saver for Vegemite lovers
everywhere, who can't eat the original thing!

135 g (5 oz/½ cup) black tahini
80 ml (2½ fl oz/⅓ cup) tamari
20 g (¾ oz/⅓ cup) nutritional yeast flakes

½ teaspoon raw honey
2 teaspoons coconut cream

Combine all the ingredients in a mixing bowl and stir until combined.

Place in a sterilised jar (see page 11) and keep in the fridge for up to 2 weeks.
Spread on toast, crackers or whatever you please!

SEEDED BUCKWHEAT BREAD

MAKES ABOUT 12 SLICES
Preparation time: 10 minutes, plus 4 hours soaking
Cooking time: 2 hours

I've never been one to say 'I don't really eat/like bread'. Those words have just never come out of my mouth, even though I'm a coeliac. This seeded bread is nut-free and awesome for breakfast with home-made healthymite (see page 43) and cashew cheese (see page 58). You can also have it with the faux-rerro rocher spread (see opposite)!

175 g (6 oz/1 cup) buckwheat, soaked for at least 2 hours, drained and rinsed

145 g (5 oz) sunflower seeds

70 g (2½ oz/½ cup) pepitas (pumpkin seeds)

90 g (3 oz/½ cup) linseeds (flax seeds)

40 g (1½ oz/¼ cup) white or black chia seeds

40 g (1½ oz/⅓ cup) hemp seeds (optional)

2½ tablespoons sesame seeds

30 g (1 oz/⅓ cup) psyllium husk

60 ml (2 fl oz/¼ cup) coconut oil

1 tablespoon nutritional yeast flakes (optional)

1 teaspoon salt

¼ teaspoon freshly ground black pepper (optional)

625 ml (21 fl oz/2½ cups) water

Line the base and sides of a 22.5 x 12.5 cm (9 x 5 in) loaf (bar) tin with baking paper.

Place all the ingredients in a large bowl and mix to combine well. Transfer to the lined tin, smoothing the surface so it is even then cover and stand for 4 hours, or until the mixture absorbs the liquid and binds together. Half an hour before you want to bake the bread, preheat the oven to 170°C (340°F).

Bake the bread for 1 hour, or until firm and golden, turn out onto a baking tray and bake for a further 1 hour, or until it sounds hollow when tapped.

Remove from the oven and allow to cool completely before slicing.

Store in an airtight container for up to 1 week, or freeze for up to 2 months.

FAUX-RERRO ROCHER SPREAD

MAKES 450 G (1 LB/2 CUPS)
Preparation time: 10 minutes

This spread is so good. It's great on seeded bread, it's great on crackers, it's great eaten
by the spoon – it's great on everything!

140 g (5 oz/1 cup) raw or activated
hazelnuts (see page 11)
155 g (5½ oz/1 cup) raw or activated
almonds (see page 11)

60 ml (2 fl oz/¼ cup) coconut nectar
60 ml (2 fl oz/¼ cup) coconut oil
30 g (1 oz/¼ cup) raw cacao powder
pinch sea salt flakes

Place all the ingredients in your food processor or blender then process until
everything is completely smooth. Transfer to a sterilised jar (see page 11) and store
in the fridge; this will keep for up to 3 weeks.

SWEET POTATO, MILLET & KALE PATTIES

MAKES 14
Preparation time: 10 minutes
Cooking time: 30 minutes

These bite-sized patties are really simple to prepare and they make the best lunch ever, especially when served with salad. Freeze them after cooking and just grab a few when you need something quick to eat, or eat them fresh in a wrap, a sandwich or in a pitta pocket.

500 g (1 lb 2 oz) orange sweet potato, peeled and diced

100 g (3½ oz/½ cup) millet

5 kale leaves, stems removed and finely chopped (about 2 cups)

2 spring onions (scallions), trimmed and finely chopped

1 tablespoon finely chopped flat-leaf (Italian) parsley

2–3 thyme sprigs, leaved picked

2 garlic cloves, crushed

sea salt and freshly ground black pepper, to taste

2 tablespoons coconut or grapeseed oil, for frying

Cook the sweet potato in a steamer basket over boiling water for about 12 minutes until tender.

Meanwhile, combine the millet with 375 ml (12½ oz/1½ cups) water in a medium saucepan then cook, uncovered, over medium–low heat for about 15 minutes or until the water has been absorbed. Remove from the heat then let the millet cool a little.

Place the remaining ingredients, except the oil, in a large bowl. Add the sweet potato and gently mash it to lightly break it up; the kale should wilt a little. Add the millet and stir until combined.

Take 70 g (2½ oz/scant ¼ cup) of the mixture at a time and make it into patties about 6 cm (2½ in) across. Heat the oil in a large, non-stick frying pan over medium heat, add the patties and cook for 2–3 minutes on each side or until golden. Serve with salad, in pockets, in wraps or on sandwiches. Or, cool and store in an airtight container in the fridge for up to 4 days, to grab when you need a little savoury snack!

INDIAN CAULIFLOWER 'RICE' PATTIES

MAKES 15
Preparation time: 25 minutes
Cooking time: 25 minutes

These patties are amazing, with their subtle coconut and curry flavours. They can be eaten straight away, or kept in the fridge and used as an anytime snack.

300 g (10½ oz) cauliflower, chopped (about ½ small cauliflower)
2½ tablespoons coconut oil
1 onion, finely chopped
3–4 teaspoons curry powder
1 garlic clove, crushed
1½ teaspoons finely grated fresh ginger
1 green chilli, seeds removed, finely chopped (optional)

50 g (1¾ oz/⅓ cup) poppy seeds
200 g (7 oz) finely chopped cabbage
45 g (1½ oz/½ cup) desiccated coconut
250 ml (8½ fl oz/1 cup) coconut cream
65 g (2¼ oz/½ cup) shelled baby peas
70 g (2½ oz) coconut flour
2½ tablespoons linseed (flax seed) meal
sea salt and freshly ground black pepper, to taste

Place the cauliflower in your food processor then, using the pulse button, pulse until it's finely chopped and resembles rice. Set aside.

Heat 1 tablespoon of the coconut oil in a large frying pan over medium heat. Add the onion, curry powder, garlic, ginger and chilli. Cook, stirring often, for 3 minutes or until the onion has softened. Add the poppy seeds and cook for a further 1–2 minutes, or until the onion is translucent and the poppy seeds begin to 'pop'.

Add 60 ml (2 fl oz/¼ cup) water, the cabbage, desiccated coconut, coconut cream and cauliflower and cook, uncovered, for 5 minutes or until the vegetables have softened.

Transfer to a mixing bowl then stir in the remaining ingredients, except the remaining oil. Take about 75 g (2¾ oz/⅓ cup) of the mixture at a time and form into patties about 7 cm (2¾ in) across.

In a clean frying pan, heat the remaining oil over medium heat. Add the patties, in batches if necessary, and cook for 3–4 minutes on each side, or until golden. Serve them straight away or let them cool and store in an airtight container in the fridge for little savoury snacks.

NOTE
Currants and slivered almonds can be added to this recipe for even more texture and flavour!

BLACK BEAN & RICE MEXI BURGERS

MAKES 15
Preparation time: 10 minutes
Cooking time: 1 hour

I love Mexican food; I love black beans and I love rice. These burgers have a definite Mexican lean and they're filled with goodness. Enough said.

140 g (5 oz/⅔ cup) short-grain brown rice

400 g (14 oz) tin black beans, drained and rinsed

2 spring onions (scallions), trimmed and finely chopped, plus extra to serve

1 small green capsicum (bell pepper), trimmed, seeded and roughly chopped

1 jalapeño chilli, finely chopped (optional)

small handful coriander (cilantro) leaves, roughly chopped

1 teaspoon ground cumin

½ teaspoon paprika

¼ teaspoon crushed garlic

15 g (½ oz/¼ cup) nutritional yeast flakes

2½ tablespoons psyllium husk

2½ tablespoons tomato paste (concentrated puree)

sea salt and freshly ground black pepper, to taste

2½ tablespoons coconut oil or grapeseed oil, for frying

chard leaves, sliced avocado, lime wedges and micro greens, to serve

Place the rice in a sieve then rinse it under cold water until the water runs clear. Combine the rice in a saucepan with 375 ml (12½ fl oz/1½ cups) water and bring it to a simmer. Cover the pan then cook the rice over medium-low heat for 40 minutes or until the water has been absorbed. Remove the pan from the heat and allow the rice to cool, uncovered.

Place all the remaining ingredients, except the oil, into your food processor and process until the vegetables are finely chopped and the beans are smooth.

Transfer the mixture to a bowl and stir in the cooled rice.

Taking 55 g (2 oz/¼ cup) of the mixture at a time, make patties about 5.5 cm (2¼ in) across. I find it easier to do this if my hands are a bit wet so the rice doesn't stick. Heat the oil in a large non-stick frying pan over medium heat then cook the patties, in batches, for 3–4 minutes on each side or until crisp and golden. Alternatively, you can bake them in a preheated 180°C (350°F) oven on a tray lined with baking paper for 25 minutes, turning them halfway through cooking. Serve straight away in chard leaves for wrapping, with avocado slices, micro greens and lime wedges for squeezing.

NOTE
If you prefer, you can use sushi rice instead of the brown rice. In this case, cook it in 340 ml (11½ fl oz/1⅓ cups) water for 15 minutes.

CHICKPEA & KIMCHI MINI PANCAKES

MAKES 8
Preparation time: 15 minutes
Cooking time: 25 minutes

My obsession with fermented foods is almost too extreme. I love them all and
I especially love the spicy flavours of kimchi. These chickpea pancakes are so easy
to make and are really healthy. They're The Absolute Best when served in lettuce cups
with tomatoes, sliced onion and other veggies of choice, or just with heaps of salad!

KIMCHI PANCAKES

225 g (8 oz/1½ cups) kimchi, roughly
  chopped

2 spring onions (scallions), trimmed and
  finely chopped, plus extra to serve

55 g (2 oz/½ cup) besan (chickpea flour)

¼ teaspoon bicarbonate of soda
  (baking soda)

sea salt and freshly ground black pepper,
  to taste

coconut or grapeseed oil, for frying

CASHEW AIOLI

155 g (5½ oz/1 cup) raw cashews

2 garlic cloves, crushed

2 teaspoons apple cider vinegar

2½ tablespoons lemon juice

100 ml (3½ fl oz) water

sea salt and freshly ground black pepper,
  to taste

SWEET CHILLI SAUCE

125 ml (4 fl oz/½ cup) maple syrup

2½ tablespoons apple cider vinegar

2½ tablespoons water

1 tablespoon dried chilli flakes

2 teaspoons arrowroot

pinch sea salt flakes

For the kimchi pancakes, place all the ingredients, except the oil, in a mixing bowl with
60 ml (2 fl oz/¼ cup) water and stir to combine well. Set aside until ready to cook.

To make the cashew aioli, combine all the ingredients in a food processor or
blender then process until smooth and creamy.

To make the sweet chilli sauce, put all the ingredients in a small saucepan. Bring
to a simmer over medium heat and cook, stirring, for 2 minutes, or until the sauce
begins to thicken. Remove from the heat then cool to room temperature.

Heat the oil in a large frying pan over medium heat. Spoon in scant 60 ml
(2 fl oz/¼ cup) amounts to form 5 cm (2 in) pancakes, until the pan is full. Cook for
3–4 minutes on each side, or until golden. Repeat with the remaining mixture then
enjoy the pancakes straight away with the cashew aioli, sweet chilli sauce and spring
onion for scattering over.

NOTE
The aioli and chilli sauce can both be made up to 3 days ahead and stored in the
refrigerator.

FISHLESS 'TUNA' CAKES

MAKES 18
Preparation time: 25 minutes, plus 4 hours soaking
Cooking time: 25 minutes

Sunflower seed 'tuna' has become a popular thing lately, and I totally know why – it's awesome. Packed with protein and delicious in taste, it's great to spread on seed crackers, with a sandwich or just eaten with a salad. Here, I've turned it into patties. Tuna patties were something we always had as kids, and these totally take me back to those days.

quinoa flakes, ground almonds or gluten-free breadcrumbs, for coating
2½ tablespoons coconut oil or grapeseed oil, for frying

SUNFLOWER SEED 'TUNA'
125 g (4½ oz/1 cup) sunflower seeds, soaked in water overnight and drained
2½ tablespoons capers in brine, drained
½ red onion, chopped
1 teaspoon apple cider vinegar
finely grated zest and juice of 1 lemon

FISHLESS CAKES
500 g (1 lb 2 oz) white sweet potato or potato, chopped
1 tablespoon finely chopped flat-leaf (Italian) parsley
2 tablespoons finely chopped fresh dill, plus extra to serve
sea salt and freshly ground black pepper, to taste
finely grated zest and juice of 1 lemon, (optional), plus lemon wedges to serve
pea sprouts, dill sprigs and vegan mayonnaise, to serve

For the sunflower seed 'tuna', place all the ingredients in your food processor or blender. Pulse until combined and the mixture resembles a crumbly, sandwich-style 'tuna' mix.

For the fishless cakes, cook the sweet potatoes in a steamer basket over boiling water for about 15 minutes or until tender, then cool slightly. Gently mash the steamed sweet potatoes in a mixing bowl and combine with the sunflower seed 'tuna' mix, herbs, and lemon zest and juice (if using). Mix well.

Take about 45 g (1½ oz/¼ cup) of the mixture at a time and form into patties about 5 cm (2 in) across. Coat each in your coating of choice; I prefer gluten-free breadcrumbs, home-made from a good quality gluten-free bread.

Heat the oil in a large frying pan over medium heat. Cook the cakes, in batches if necessary, for 3–4 minutes on each side until golden. Enjoy straight away with pea sprouts, dill sprigs and vegan mayo, or allow to cool and store in an airtight container in the fridge, to have on hand as savoury snacks!

THAI-STYLE 'CRAB' CAKES

MAKES 7 LARGE, OR 14 SMALL, CAKES
Preparation time: 10 minutes
Cooking time: 15 minutes

––––––––––

'You wouldn't know these don't have crab in them,' is a direct quote from my dad who thought I had actually, as a vegan, put crab into my patties. These crab cakes are packed with flavour and are perfect for the lunchbox or as an on-the-go snack. They're best served with salad and home-made sweet chilli sauce (see page 51).

100 g (3½ oz/⅔ cup) gluten-free breadcrumbs, for coating

2½ tablespoons coconut oil or grapeseed oil, for frying

fresh herbs, such as Thai basil, coriander (cilantro) and mint leaves, to serve

sliced chilli, lime wedges and spring onions (scallions), to serve

'CRAB' CAKES

400 g (14 oz) tinned artichokes (220 g/ 8 oz drained weight), drained and finely chopped

finely grated zest of 1 lime (kaffir lime zest works great, but normal lime is fine)

55 g (2 oz/½ cup) besan (chickpea flour)

2–3 spring onions (scallions), trimmed and finely chopped

1 tablespoon finely chopped Thai basil or basil

1 red chilli, finely chopped

½ teaspoon finely grated fresh ginger

½ teaspoon shop-bought lemongrass paste (optional)

2½ tablespoons finely chopped coriander (cilantro) leaves

2½ tablespoons vegan mayonnaise

1 teaspoon tamari

½ teaspoon white miso paste

½ teaspoon wakame, kelp or nori powder (optional)

For the 'crab' cakes, mix all the ingredients together in a mixing bowl until they're well combined.

Take about 2 heaped tablespoons of the mixture at a time and form into 4.5 cm (1¾ in) patties. Toss each in breadcrumbs to lightly coat.

Heat the oil in a large frying pan over medium heat. Add the patties, in batches if necessary, and cook for 3–4 minutes on each side or until golden. Enjoy straight away with herbs, chilli, spring onion and lime for squeezing, or cool and store in an airtight container in the fridge to use later as little savoury snacks! They'll keep in the fridge for 2–3 days.

NOTE
If artichokes are not drained well, more chickpea (besan) flour may be required.

MUSHROOM & THYME ARANCINI BALLS

MAKES 10
Preparation time: 15 minutes
Cooking time: 40 minutes

The Italians' snack game has always been strong, and the arancini ball is a great example of that. These balls are so awesome eaten as soon as they have been cooked, and also the next day as a delicious snack on-the-go.

2½ tablespoons grapeseed or coconut oil, plus extra for cooking
1 onion, finely chopped
3 garlic cloves, crushed
220 g (8 oz/1 cup) arborio rice
250 ml (8½ fl oz/1 cup) white wine
sea salt and freshly ground black pepper, to taste
1 tablespoon nutritional yeast flakes
¼ teaspoon garlic powder
¼ teaspoon onion powder
3 thyme sprigs
250 ml (8½ fl oz/1 cup) water

MUSHROOM FILLING
1 tablespoon grapeseed or coconut oil
100 g (3½ oz) brown or portobello mushrooms chopped
2 thyme sprigs, leaves picked
sea salt and freshly ground black pepper, to taste

COATING
35 g (1¼ oz/⅓ cup) besan (chickpea flour)
125 ml (4½ fl oz/½ cup) almond milk
60 g (2 oz/½ cup) gluten-free breadcrumbs

Heat a frying pan over medium heat. Add the oil, onion and garlic and cook, stirring, for 2–3 minutes or until the onion is translucent. Add the rice and allow it to cook for another 2 minutes. Add the wine, stirring until it has been absorbed. Add the salt and pepper, yeast flakes, garlic powder, onion powder and thyme. Gradually add the water, a little at a time, stirring until all the liquid has been absorbed before adding more. Cook, stirring, for about 15 minutes. Remove from the heat and allow to cool. Remove the thyme sprigs.

To make the mushroom filling, heat the oil in a frying pan over medium heat. Add the mushrooms and thyme leaves and cook for 3–4 minutes, stirring often, or until the mushrooms have softened. Remove from the heat, season to taste and allow to cool.

Take 1–2 tablespoons of the rice in the palm of your hand and roll it to form a ball. Push your finger into the ball to form a large hole for the filling, then add about 1 teaspoon of the mushroom mixture to the hole. Press some of the rice ball over the hole to enclose the filling. Roll each ball in the besan, dip in almond milk to lightly coat, then finally roll in the breadcrumbs. Heat the extra oil in a large frying pan over a medium heat. Fry the arancini in batches until golden. Alternatively, bake them in a 180°C (350°F) oven for 15 minutes, or until golden. Serve hot.

CASHEW CHEESE BALLS

MAKES 5–10
Preparation time: 10 minutes, plus 4 hours soaking
Setting time: about 3 hours

I practically live off cashew cheese. I have it for breakfast on my toast or seed crackers, I have it in my salad for lunch, and it's virtually always used in some form in my dinner. These balls not only look great, they are perfect for serving with crackers when friends drop by. Keep these in a jar, submerged in olive oil, to keep them livin' for longer.

155 g (5½ oz/1 cup) raw cashews, soaked for at least 4 hours, drained and rinsed
1 teaspoon white miso paste
1 tablespoon nutritional yeast flakes
1 tablespoon lemon juice
1 tablespoon coconut oil
¼ teaspoon apple cider vinegar
pinch sea salt, or to taste

COATING SUGGESTIONS
crushed pistachios, herbs and spring onions (scallions)
lemon zest and dill
za'atar spice
dukkah
dried chilli flakes
crushed nuts or seeds

Place the cashews, miso, yeast flakes, lemon juice, coconut oil and cider vinegar in your food processor or blender and blend until completely smooth. Season with salt to taste.

Take about a tablespoon of the mixture at a time and place it in the middle of a small-ish piece of plastic wrap; use double the amount of mixture to make bigger balls. Bring the plastic wrap up and around the mixture to form a neat ball then tie the plastic wrap tightly to secure. Place on a tray and refrigerate for at least 3 hours, or until firm. Unwrap the balls then roll them in the coating of your choice.

Serve the cashew cheese balls with Mega seed crackers (see page 42) or a good quality gluten-free bread. These will keep for up to a week in the fridge in a sterilised jar (see page 11) submerged in olive oil, and a couple of months in the freezer.

NOTE
If freezing, remove them from the freezer to thaw about 20 minutes before serving.

RAINBOW SUSHI BALLS

MAKES 16
Preparation time: 10 minutes
Cooking time: 30 minutes

These sushi balls are soooo cute and they are also insanely perfect for munching when on the go. They're also really good in lunchboxes. You can really play around with the fillings according to what you like; keep these simple using just chopped raw veggies, as suggested below, or add the tofu–mushroom mix for a touch more flavour.

440 g (15½ oz/2 cups) sushi rice (koshihikari rice)

7 nori sheets, torn

2½ tablespoons sesame seeds, plus extra for coating (optional)

100 g (3½ oz) firm or pressed tofu, chopped

30 g (1 oz/½ cup) chopped shiitake, oyster or brown mushrooms

1 teaspoon freshly grated ginger

1 teaspoon coconut oil

2 teaspoons tamari

other fillings: finely chopped avocado, carrot, cucumber, red capsicum (bell pepper), red cabbage, spring onions (scallions)

pickled ginger and tamari, to serve (optional)

Place the rice in a sieve then rinse it until the water runs clear. Place in a saucepan with 500 ml (17 fl oz/2 cups) water then bring to a simmer over medium–high heat. Cover the pan tightly, reduce the heat to low then cook for 20 minutes or until the water has been absorbed. Remove from the heat then stand, covered, until the rice has cooled to room temperature.

Place the torn nori into a small food processor or bullet blender and process until a fine powder forms. Stir the nori and sesame seeds through the rice. Set aside.

Cook the tofu, mushrooms and ginger with the coconut oil in a small frying pan over medium heat for 5 minutes, or until the mushrooms have softened. Add the tamari and cook for another 3–4 minutes. Remove from the heat.

Take about 90 g (3 oz/⅓ cup) of the rice at a time and lay it out on your hand, pressing it evenly to form a disc about 5.5 cm (2¼ in)across. Place about 1 teaspoon of your choice of filling ingredients in the middle of the disc then use your hand to bring the rice over the filling, enclosing it to form a sealed ball.

Roll each ball in additional sesame seeds if you like, then serve with pickled ginger and tamari if desired. Pop these in the fridge until serving; they're best eaten within 2 days.

WHITE BEAN, BROCCOLI & QUINOA PATTIES

MAKES 15
Preparation time: 10 minutes
Cooking time: 45 minutes

This is a simple pattie recipe, but a good one. Bursting with lemony flavour and full of protein, these are a great savoury snack to include in your work or school lunchbox. When served with salad, or in a wrap, these are totally the bomb. They're also good with hummus, or any other delish dip you happen to love and have around.

gluten-free breadcrumbs, for coating

2½ tablespoons coconut oil or grapeseed oil, for frying

PATTIES

100 g (3½ oz/½ cup) quinoa

400 g (14 oz) tin cannellini (lima) beans, drained and rinsed

200 g (7 oz) broccoli, steamed, cooled and roughly chopped

¼ red onion, roughly chopped

2½ tablespoons nutritional yeast flakes

finely grated zest of 1 lemon

2½ tablespoons lemon juice

2 tablespoons linseed (flax seed) meal

1 tablespoon finely chopped mint

1 tablespoon finely chopped flat-leaf (Italian) parsley

sea salt and freshy ground black pepper, to taste

1 teaspoon dried chilli flakes (optional)

For the patties, place the quinoa in a sieve then rinse under cold water until it runs clear. Place it in a saucepan with 250 ml (8½ fl oz/1 cup) water and bring it to the boil over medium heat. Cover the pan and cook for 20 minutes or until the water has been absorbed. Set aside to cool.

Place the beans, broccoli and onion in your food processor or blender then pulse until combined.

Transfer the mixture to a mixing bowl with the quinoa and remaining ingredients. Set aside for 20 minutes; this allows the linseed meal to bind everything together.

Take about 60 g (2 oz/⅓ cup) of the mixture at a time and form them into patties about 5 cm (2 in) across. Toss the patties into the breadcrumbs to lightly coat them.

Heat the oil in a large frying pan over medium heat. Add the patties, in batches if necessary, and cook for 3–4 minutes on each side or until golden. Enjoy straight away or cool and store in an airtight container in the fridge for up to 3 days, for little savoury snacks!

N° 3

SWEET TOOTH

SERIOUSLY THE BEST 'TOBLERONE' BLISS BALLS

MAKES 14
Preparation time: 10 minutes

———————

I'm not lying. These are probably my favourite thing in this entire cookbook. They are just seriously The Best Thing Ever. If you like chocolate, crunch and truffle-like mouthfuls, I'm pretty sure you too will quickly become obsessed with these.

235 g (8½ oz/1½ cups) roasted almonds
80 g (2¾ oz/½ cup) unsalted
  roasted peanuts
2½ tablespoons almond butter
2½ tablespoons raw honey or 2 tablespoons
  rice malt syrup

4 medjool dates (about 80 g/2¾ oz), pitted
30 g (1 oz/¼ cup) raw cacao powder
3 tablespoons coconut sugar
100 g (3½ oz) raw milk chocolate, melted
  and cooled

Place all the ingredients in your food processor or blender and process until they're finely chopped and well combined. (Don't whizz them too much as you still want that slight Toblerone crunch and texture from the nuts.)

Take about a tablespoon of the mixture at a time and roll it into 2.5 cm (1 in) balls. Place the balls in an airtight container in the fridge or freezer. These will keep for up to 2 weeks in the fridge, and a couple of months in the freezer.

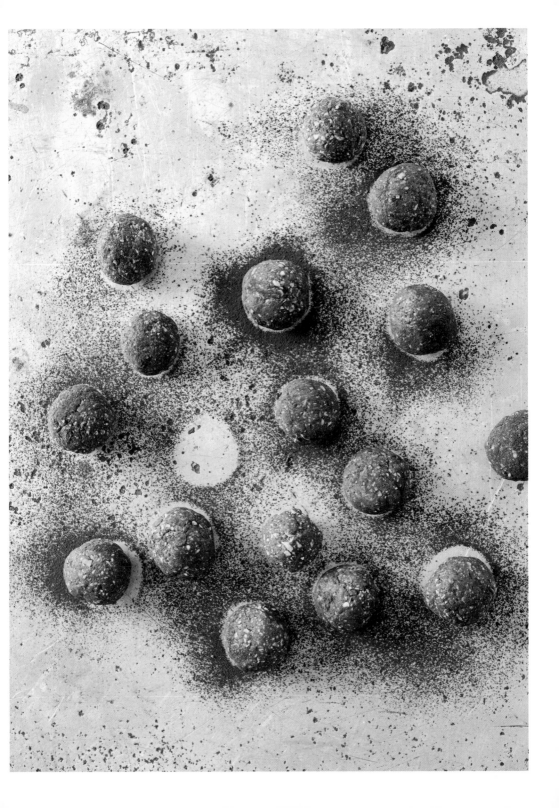

GOLDEN FUN-TIME BLISS BALLS

MAKES 16
Preparation time: 10 minutes

———————

If you have never eaten the classic Australian ice cream, the Golden Gaytime, I can tell you one thing – it leaves other ice creams in the shade. Although it's been a good million years since I ate one myself, I have fond memories of them and these balls instantly bring those memories flooding back. The buckwheat on the outside is reminiscent of the cookie crunch of the Gaytime, and the super delicious centre reminds me of that caramel-vanilla ice cream you get inside. If you wanted to make these even more deluxe, you could dip the balls in raw melted chocolate before rolling them in the buckwheat. Insane.

12 medjool dates (about 240 g/8½ oz), pitted

40 g (1¼ oz/⅓ cup) vanilla flavoured plant-based protein powder

½ teaspoon ground cinnamon (optional)

90 g (3 oz/⅓ cup) nut butter, toasted coconut butter or seed butter

2 tablespoons caramelised buckwheat, plus extra for coating

2 tablespoons raw honey or maple syrup

Place the dates, protein powder, cinnamon (if using), nut butter, caramelised buckwheat and raw honey in your food processor or blender. Pulse until they're combined.

Take about a tablespoon of the mixture at a time and roll into 3.5 cm (1½ in) balls then roll in caramelised buckwheat to lightly coat. Place the balls in an airtight container then put them in the fridge or freezer. These will keep for up to 2 weeks in the fridge, and a couple of months in the freezer.

RASPBERRY RIPE TRUFFLES

MAKES 18
Preparation time: 10 minutes

I was never a fan of the Cherry Ripe chocolate bar, a very sweet mash-up of coconut, glacé (candied) cherries and chocolate. But these, I am totally down for. They're the perfect combination of tangy raspberry and sweet coconut and they never fail to go down a treat.

FILLING
180 g (6½ oz/2 cups) desiccated coconut
100 g (3½ oz/⅔ cup) dried raspberries
1½ tablespoons raspberry powder
60 ml (2 fl oz/¼ cup) rice malt syrup
2½ tablespoons coconut butter
½ teaspoon vanilla extract

COATING
150 g (5½ oz) raw dark chocolate, melted and cooled

Place all the filling ingredients in your food processor or blender and pulse together until they're chopped and well combined.

Line a tray with baking paper. Take about a tablespoon of the mixture at a time and roll it into 1.5 cm (½ in) balls. Dip each ball into the melted chocolate to coat completely, draining off any excess chocolate. Place the balls on the tray then refrigerate until the chocolate has set. Store them in an airtight container in the fridge or the freezer. These will keep for up to 2 weeks in the fridge, and a couple of months in the freezer.

ANZAC BISCUIT BALLS

MAKES 15
Preparation time: 10 minutes

Here's a tribute to Australia's and New Zealand's ANZAC soldiers, and the biscuit (cookie) of the same name that we all go so nuts for, Downunder. These are perfect for both lunchboxes and for keeping the cookie monster inside you at bay – at any time of the day (or night).

2 tablespoons coconut oil

80 g (2¾ oz/½ cup) roasted or activated cashews (see page 11)

110 g (4 oz/¾ cup) crushed pistachios

50 g (1¾ oz/½ cup) gluten-free rolled oats, rolled buckwheat or quinoa flakes

2½ tablespoons peanut butter

90 g (3 oz/1 cup) desiccated coconut

90 g (3 oz/¼ cup) maple syrup

3 teaspoons raw honey

Place all the ingredients in your food processor or blender and process until everything is finely chopped and combined.

Take about a tablespoon of the mixture at a time and roll it into 2.5 cm (1 in) balls. Place them in an airtight container then refrigerate or freeze. These will keep for up to 2 weeks in the fridge, and a couple of months in the freezer.

'ROLOS' WITH MY HOMIES

MAKES 18
Preparation time: 15 minutes, plus 30 minutes setting

Hot dang these are good. Perfect caramel goodness coated in raw dark chocolate.
I don't know about you, but I think that's a pretty winning combination and anyone
who eats these will fall in love with you, instantly.* These balls are a great substitute for
dessert when you want something sweet, but nothing too full-on. Plus, they have what
I call the 'pimp my bliss ball' factor, where you can add a few extra powders (see note)
for added goodness. Or you can just go with what's here, for a simpler treat. These can
be made nut-free by substituting the nut butter with tahini, and cacao-free by using
a carob bar to melt and coat, instead of the chocolate.

*Don't hold me to that.

CARAMEL FILLING
10 medjool dates (about 200 g/7 oz), pitted

2 tablespoons maple syrup

90 g (3 oz/⅓ cup) almond butter, cashew
butter or tahini

1 teaspoon vanilla extract or ½ teaspoon
vanilla powder

1 tablespoon golden linseed (flax seed) meal

1 tablespoon coconut butter or coconut
paste (optional)

pinch pink sea salt flakes

COATING
100 g (3½ oz) raw dark chocolate, melted
and cooled, or 1 serving raw chocolate,
melted and cooled (see page 135)

Place all the filling ingredients in your food processor or blender and pulse until
they're well combined and the mixture forms a firm ball.

Wrap the ball in plastic wrap and put it in the fridge to set for about
30 minutes. Line a medium-sized tray with baking paper.

When the date mixture is firm, take about half a tablespoon of it at a time and
roll them into 1 cm (½ in) balls. Dip the balls in the melted chocolate, allowing any
excess chocolate to drain off, and place them on the tray. Put them in the fridge for
the chocolate to set then transfer them to an airtight container. Store them in either
the fridge or freezer; they will keep for up to 2 weeks in the fridge, and a couple of
months in the freezer.

NOTE
You can add one (or all) of the following when making your caramel filling: 1 teaspoon
maca powder, 1 teaspoon mesquite powder and/or 1 teaspoon lucuma powder.

NOT-SO-MALT TEASERS

MAKES 10
Preparation time: 15 minutes

———————

I miss Maltesers on a daily basis. They were awesome. Before I knew I was a coeliac sufferer, they were my chocolate of choice. They're crunchy, tasty and just the perfect size. Sigh. But here's a good alternative I developed and, while maybe not the healthiest recipe in the book, these are a total treat when you need one.

80 g (2¾ oz/½ cup) macadamia nuts or roasted almonds
80 g (2¾ oz/½ cup) roasted peanuts
100 g (3½ oz) cashew butter
2½ tablespoons raw honey

2 tablespoons rice malt syrup
1 teaspoon vanilla extract
80 g (2¾ oz) raw dark chocolate, melted and cooled

Place all the ingredients except the melted chocolate in your food processor or blender and pulse together until well combined.

Line a small tray with baking paper. Taking about a tablespoon of the mixture at a time, roll the mixture into 1.5 cm (½ in) balls. Dip each ball in the melted chocolate to coat, allowing any excess chocolate to drain off, then put them on the tray. Refrigerate until the chocolate has set then transfer balls to an airtight container. Store them in the fridge or the freezer; they'll keep for up to 2 weeks in the fridge, and a couple of months in the freezer.

LAMINGTON BLISS BALLS

MAKES 18
Preparation time: 25 minutes, plus 30 minutes setting

Australians love lamingtons – it's an iconic national cake-dessert that was developed in the late 1800s in Queensland (fun fact!). This raw bliss ball adaptation is packed with healthy fats and antioxidants that arguably make these a better way to enjoy this nostalgic favourite. Everybody loves a lamo'! (Which is Australian for lamington. Down here, we like to shorten our words.)

COCONUT MIXTURE
160 g (5½ oz/1 cup) macadamia nuts
180 g (6½ oz/2 cups) desiccated coconut
80 ml (2½ fl oz/⅓ cup) maple syrup
60 ml (2 fl oz/¼ cup) coconut oil

FILLING
40 g (1½ oz) chia jam or refined sugar-free raspberry jam

COATING
100 g (3½ oz) dark chocolate, melted and cooled
90 g (3 oz/1 cup) dessicated coconut

To make the coconut mixture, combine the macadamia nuts, coconut, maple syrup and coconut oil in your food processor and process until smooth.

Line a baking tray with baking paper. Take about a tablespoon of the coconut mixture at a time and roll it into 2.5 cm (1 in) balls. Working with one at a time, flatten each ball in your hand into a circle that's about 5 cm (2 in) across. Blob ½ teaspoon of the jam into the middle then close the circle around the jam, squeezing the joins gently together so it can't get out. Gently re-roll the whole thing into a neat ball. Place each ball on the tray then refrigerate (or freeze) them for about 30 minutes, or until they firm up.

Dip the balls in the chocolate, allowing any excess chocolate to drain off then roll each ball in the coconut to lightly coat. Return them to the fridge or freezer on the tray for the chocolate to set then, once it's set, transfer the balls to an airtight container and refrigerate or freeze them. These will keep for up to 2 weeks in the fridge, and a couple of months in the freezer.

NOTE
For an alternative coating, combine 50 g (1¾ oz) melted cacao butter or coconut oil, 1 tablespoon raw cacao powder and 1 tablespoon maple syrup in a bowl and dip the balls in this before coating in desiccated coconut. You'll need around 90 g (3 oz/1 cup) of coconut.

TURKISH DELIGHT BLISS BALLS

MAKES 18
Preparation time: 10 minutes

_____

These balls are inspired by my partner's Turkish family, who make so many delicious things that I can't eat (but I so want to eat!), because of my allergies. These taste delicious, look good and are as sweet as my beautiful Turkish in-laws.

3 teaspoons rosewater
200 g (7 oz/1⅓ cups) dried cranberries
50 g (1¾ oz/¾ cup) dried barberries or 50 g (1¾ oz/½ cup) goji berries
4 medjool dates (about 80 g/2¾ oz), pitted

2½ tablespoons raw honey or maple syrup
150 g (5½ oz/1 cup) pistachio nuts, plus 50 g (1¾ oz/⅓ cup) crushed pistachio nuts for coating
50 g (1¾ oz/⅓ cup) linseed (flax seed) meal

Place all the ingredients, except the crushed pistachio nuts, into your food processor or blender and pulse them together until combined.

Take about a tablespoon of the mixture at a time and roll it into 2.5 cm (1 in) balls. Roll each in the crushed pistachios to lightly coat, then place the balls in an airtight container. Refrigerate or freeze them; these will keep for up to 2 weeks in the fridge, and a couple of months in the freezer.

COCONUT ROUGH RIDER BALLS

MAKES 12
Preparation time: 10 minutes
Cooking time: 5 minutes

Stop, drop, blitz 'em up, roll 'em up... that's how (coconut) rough riders roll. An ode to DMX, the original rough rider, these balls are stupidly good. Try them for yourself and then you'll believe me. These can be made nut-free by substituting the cashew butter with a seed butter; I like to use a creamy sunflower seed butter.

90 g (3 oz/1 cup) desiccated coconut
2 tablespoons raw cacao powder
1 tablespoon coconut butter
1 tablespoon raw cashew butter

1 tablespoon raw honey
2 tablespoons lucuma powder
6 medjool dates (about 120 g/4½ oz), pitted

Preheat the oven to 180°C (350°F). Spread the coconut on a tray and toast it for 5 minutes or so – just until it starts to turn a little golden. Cool it to room temperature then put it, with the rest of the ingredients, into your food processor or blender and pulse together until combined.

Take about a tablespoon of the mixture at a time and roll it into 2.5 cm (1 in) balls. Place these in a single layer in an airtight container then refrigerate or freeze them. These will keep for up to 2 weeks in the fridge, and a couple of months in the freezer.

PEANUT BUTTER TRUFFLES

MAKES 18
Preparation time: 10 minutes

There is not too much to say about these. Peanut butter. Chocolate. Salt. Have I sold you on them yet? If you like, you can sprinkle a few sea salt flakes onto each one after you've dipped them in chocolate – it makes them look even lovelier.

160 g (5½ oz/1 cup) dry-roasted peanuts
100 g (3½ oz) crunchy peanut butter
90 g (3 oz/¼ cup) raw honey, maple syrup
    or rice malt syrup

1 tablespoon maple syrup
½ teaspoon salt
100 g (3½ oz) raw, dark chocolate,
    melted and cooled

Place all the ingredients, except the melted chocolate, in your food processor or blender and pulse together until everything is combined.

    Line a tray with baking paper. Take about a tablespoon of the mixture at a time and roll it into 1.5 cm (½ in) balls. Dip each ball into the melted chocolate, allowing any excess to drain off. Refrigerate the balls until the chocolate has set then transfer them to an airtight container and store in the refrigerator or freezer. These will keep for up to 2 weeks in the fridge, and a couple of months in the freezer.

RED VELVET BEET BITES

MAKES 12
Preparation time: 10 minutes

Yassss queen! Another treat which sneaks in some veg! You would never know these bliss balls contain beetroot, but they do. These are light and cake-like, and are so inviting, with their beautiful red colour. Because they contain raw vegetable, they won't last as long as other bliss balls do so consume them within a few days, or throw them in the freezer to keep them longer.

½ medium beetroot (beet) (about 100 g/ 3½ oz), peeled and grated
180 g (6½ oz/2 cups) desiccated coconut
2 tablespoons raw cacao powder
1 teaspoon vanilla extract

8 medjool dates (about 160 g/5½ oz), pitted
pinch sea salt flakes
extra raw cacao powder or desiccated coconut, for coating

Place all the ingredients, except the coconut or cacao for coating, into your food processor or blender. Pulse them together until combined.

Take about a tablespoon of the mixture at a time and roll it into 2.5 cm (1 in) balls. Spread the coating of your choice on a plate and roll the balls in that, to lightly coat. Place the balls in an airtight container and refrigerate or freeze them. These will keep for up to 1 week in the fridge, and a couple of months in the freezer.

FAUX-RERRO ROCHER HAZELNUT BLISS BALLS

MAKES 14
Preparation time: 20 minutes

Here's a perfect treat for choccy addicts looking to satisfy their sweet cravings. This re-creation of a classic dessert is a healthier option, packed with goodies for the heart and brain, such as raw cacao and hazelnuts. Whip them up as a special gift for someone you love, or simply enjoy yourself.

FILLING
150 g (5½ oz) hazelnuts
9 medjool dates (about 180 g/6½ oz), pitted
30 g (1 oz/¼ cup) raw cacao powder
40 g (1½ oz) hazelnut or almond butter
14 hazelnuts, roasted and peeled

COATING
50 g (1¾ oz) cacao butter
1½ tablespoons raw cacao powder
1 tablespoon maple syrup
75 g (2¾ oz/½ cup) roasted, peeled hazelnuts, crushed

Place all the filling ingredients, except the 14 roasted hazelnuts, in your food processor or blender and pulse together until combined.

Line a tray with baking paper. Take about a tablespoon of the mixture at a time and roll it into 2.5 cm (1 in) balls, pushing a roasted hazelnut into the centre of each ball. Place the balls on the tray.

Meanwhile, to make the coating, melt the cacao butter in a double boiler set over simmering water. Add the raw cacao powder and maple syrup and whisk everything together until combined and smooth. Cool the mixture.

Dip the balls into the chocolate mixture, place them on the tray and set aside until the chocolate has set. Repeat the process 2–3 times or until the balls have a thick coating. Before the final coating sets, roll each ball in the crushed hazelnuts to lightly coat, then return to the tray. Refrigerate for around 10 minutes or until the chocolate has set firmly.

Transfer the balls to an airtight container and refrigerate or freeze. These will keep for up to 2 weeks in the fridge, and a couple of months in the freezer.

NOTE
You can use 2½ tablespoons of coconut oil in the coating instead of the cacao butter. Even easier, you can replace the whole lot with 100 g (3½ oz) cooled, melted raw dark chocolate and use this to coat the balls instead of the mixture above. Roll them in the hazelnuts, as per the recipe.

CHOCOLATE CRACKLES

MAKES 12
Preparation time: 10 minutes

Chocolate crackles. More like chocolate CRACK; am I right? These are so tasty you will be dribbling for more at the refrigerator door. And I'm sorry if I have started a new addiction here, but these are just a great way to enjoy an old childhood classic.

60 g (2 oz/¼ cup) almond butter
90 g (3 oz/¼ cup) raw honey
40 g (1½ oz/⅓ cup) raw cacao powder
30 g (1 oz/⅓ cup) desiccated coconut

2 tablespoons coconut oil
1 teaspoon vanilla extract
55 g (2 oz/1¾ cups) unsweetened brown rice crisps or rice puffs

Combine all the ingredients in a mixing bowl and stir together until combined.

Take about a tablespoon of the mixture at a time and roll it into 2.5 cm (1 in) balls. Place the balls in an airtight container then refrigerate or freeze them. These will keep for up to 2 weeks in the fridge, and a couple of months in the freezer.

NOTE
I use brown rice crisps for these. If you use rice puffs instead, you'll end up with about 24 balls as the puffs are bigger than crisps.

BAKLAVA BLISS BALLS

MAKES 16
Preparation time: 10 minutes

Another nod to the Turkish side of my partner's family, these baklava balls are not quite
the real thing, admittedly. But they are still awesomely delicious and they totally have
the general vibes of baklava. Namely, they're sweet, nutty and filled with goodness.

155 g (5½ oz/1 cup) almonds
100 g (3½ oz/⅔ cup) pistachio nuts
150 g (5½ oz/1½ cups) walnut halves
1 teaspoon ground cinnamon
pinch ground cloves

¼ teaspoon orange blossom water or
rose water
175 g (6 oz/½ cup) raw honey
1 tablespoon finely grated lemon zest

Place the almonds, pistachio nuts and walnuts in your food processor or blender
and pulse until the nuts are all roughly broken up. Add the cinnamon, cloves, orange
blossom water, honey and lemon zest and blend until the mixture is combined and
comes together.

Take about a tablespoon of the mixture at a time and roll it into 2.5 cm (1 in)
balls. Place them in an airtight container and refrigerate or freeze them. These will
keep for up to 2 weeks in the fridge, and a couple of months in the freezer.

NOTE
If you like, sprinkle or roll these in some extra crushed pistachios straight after you
shape them into balls.

DATE NIGHT TRUFFLES

MAKES 12
Preparation time: 10 minutes

––––––––––

If ever I went on a date, and my date made me these, I would be completely over the moon. The quickest, easiest dessert to whip up, these are SO pretty and taste SO good! Sometimes it's the simplest things that really are the best.

12 medjool dates (about 240 g/8½ oz)
60 g (2 oz/¼ cup) crunchy peanut butter
100 g (3½ oz) raw dark chocolate, melted and cooled

sea salt flakes or coconut 'bacon' (see page 134)

Cut each date through the middle lengthways, using a small sharp knife. Take out the stones then gently butterfly each date out (which is a fancy way to say open each date up without tearing the ends – you want them to keep their shape). Fill each date with peanut butter then close the date around the peanut butter; it's totally fine if you overfill them a bit and your dates hardly close. They'll be even more delicious. Place them on a tray lined with baking paper then put them in the freezer for about 10 minutes or until firm.

Remove your dates from the freezer and dip each one in the melted chocolate, allowing any excess chocolate to drain off. Sprinkle the dates with a little sea salt (or some coconut 'bacon'), then put them back into the freezer for the chocolate to set.

Enjoy them immediately, straight from the freezer. Or, leave them there, in an airtight container, until you're ready to knock the socks off your loved one (or just treat yourself). They'll keep for a few months in the freezer.

Nº 4

OTHER TREATS

RAW 'TWIX' BARS

MAKES 12 (OR 24)
Preparation time: 15 minutes
Setting time: about 1 hour

There is a reason why George Costanza, in a *Seinfeld* episode, got so upset about someone eating his Twix bar. They are just so darn good you really don't want to share them. These Twixes are raw, so they're not exactly the real deal, but they are close enough for me. Keep these on hand in your freezer to snack on whenever you please – which will be always. Until you run out; in which case, just make more!

BASE

155 g (5½ oz/1 cup) activated or raw cashews or macadamia nuts (see page 11)

45 g (1½ oz/½ cup) desiccated coconut

2½ tablespoons ground almonds

½ teaspoon vanilla extract or ¼ teaspoon vanilla powder

2 tablespoons maple syrup, coconut nectar or rice malt syrup

CARAMEL

13 medjool dates (about 260 g/9 oz), pitted

60 ml (2 fl oz/¼ cup) maple syrup, coconut nectar or rice malt syrup

90 g (3 oz/⅓ cup) nut or seed butter

1 teaspoon vanilla extract or ½ teaspoon vanilla powder

1 tablespoon mesquite powder (optional)

pinch sea salt flakes

CHOCOLATE COATING

100 g (3½ oz) raw or dark chocolate, melted and cooled

Place all the ingredients for the base in your food processor and pulse until well combined.

Line the base of a 20 x 15 cm (8 x 6 in) baking tin with baking paper. Place the nut mixture in the tin, pressing it firmly and evenly over the base. Transfer to the freezer and freeze for about 30 minutes, or until firm.

To make the caramel, combine all the ingredients in the cleaned food processor and blend together until smooth. Remove the tin from the freezer and spread the caramel layer evenly over the base. Return to the freezer to set firm.

Line a small tray with baking paper.

Once the mixture is firm, remove the Twix from the tin and cut into 12 even-sized fingers. You can then cut these in half widthways, to give 24 smaller fingers, if you like. Dip the fingers into the melted chocolate, draining off any excess, and place them on the tray. Refrigerate or freeze until the chocolate has set then transfer them to an airtight container to store. These will keep, ideally frozen, for a couple of months (or 2 days, if you find them as delicious as I do!). Note that these go a bit soft in the fridge so freezer storage is best.

'BOUNTY' HUNTERS

MAKES 12
Preparation time: 15 minutes
Setting time: about 1 hour

———————

I was never a fan of coconutty, chocolate-coated Bounty bars when I was younger; to me they were just the weird chocolate we gave my mum to eat from those variety-pack mixtures. Us kids scoffed the others. Now though, I very much enjoy the combination of chocolate and coconut; maybe it's to do with becoming more mature! These are great, and really easy to make, and you (and your mum) will love them. Especially if you use a good chocolate – at least 70% cocoa solids.

FILLING
180 g (6½ oz/2 cups) desiccated coconut
1 tablespoon coconut oil
60 g (2 oz/¼ cup) coconut butter
  or coconut paste
100 ml (3½ fl oz) coconut cream

60 ml (2 fl oz/¼ cup) maple syrup,
  coconut nectar or raw honey

CHOCOLATE COATING
100 g (3½ oz) raw or dark chocolate,
  melted and cooled

Place all the filling ingredients in your food processor or blender and process until well combined.

Line the base of a 20 x 15 cm (8 x 6 in) baking tin with baking paper. Transfer the mixture to the tin and press it firmly and evenly over the base then place in the freezer for about 20 minutes, or until firm.

Line a small tray with baking paper.

Once frozen, remove the Bounty mixture from the tin and cut it into 12 even-sized fingers. Dip the fingers into the melted chocolate, draining off any excess, then place them on the tray. Refrigerate or freeze until the chocolate has set then transfer them to an airtight container to store. If you choose to freeze them, they're best consumed slightly thawed beforehand; straight from the fridge is perfect. They'll keep for 2 weeks in the fridge, and a couple of months in the freezer.

ALMOST-A-'SNICKERS' BAR

MAKES 12
Preparation time: 15 minutes
Setting time: about 1 hour

There is no eating these politely. They are just so good, you will literally inhale one quicker than you can save that 'mindful eating' quote on Pinterest. Make these now and thank me later.

BASE

155 g (5½ oz/1 cup) activated or raw cashews (see page 11)

45 g (1½ oz/½ cup) desiccated coconut

2 tablespoons maple syrup

CARAMEL

13 medjool dates (about 260 g/9 oz), pitted

60 ml (2 fl oz/¼ cup) maple syrup

90 g (3 oz/⅓ cup) peanut butter

1 teaspoon vanilla extract

pinch sea salt flakes

65 g (2¼ oz) activated almonds or peanuts, roughly chopped (see page 11)

CHOCOLATE COATING

150 g (5½ oz) raw or dark chocolate (at least 70% cocoa solids), melted and cooled

For the base, place all the ingredients in your food processor or blender and pulse together until combined.

Line the base of a 20 x 15 cm (8 x 6 in) baking tin with baking paper. Transfer the mixture to the tin and press it firmly and evenly over the base. Place it in the freezer for about 30 minutes, or until firm.

To make the caramel, combine all the ingredients in the cleaned food processor and process until smooth. Remove the base from the freezer and spread the caramel layer evenly over the base. Scatter with the almonds then return to the freezer until set.

Line a tray with baking paper.

Once frozen, remove the 'Snickers' mixture from the tin and slice into 12 even-sized bars. To coat, dip each one in the melted chocolate, allowing any excess to drain off, then place the bars on the tray. Refrigerate or freeze until they are set.

Keep these in an airtight container in the fridge or freezer and eat when you need a sweet treat. They'll keep for 2 weeks in the fridge, and 2 months in the freezer.

DOUBLE CHOC SEA SALT & HEMP SEED BROWNIES

MAKES 9 BROWNIES
Preparation time: 15 minutes
Cooking time: 25 minutes

You know what they say, 'a brownie a day keeps the frownies away!' These brownies are definitely the key to a good time. Grain-free, packed with protein (hemp seeds aren't just for hippies!), they're easily made nut-free by using a seed butter. Oh, and they're also refined sugar-free.

40 g (1½ oz/¼ cup) linseed (flax seed) meal
1 teaspoon baking powder
½ teaspoon bicarbonate of soda (baking soda)
60 g (2 oz/½ cup) raw cacao powder
80 ml (2½ fl oz/⅓ cup) maple syrup
2 tablespoons coconut nectar

1 teaspoon vanilla powder or 2 teaspoons vanilla extract
30 g (1 oz/¼ cup) arrowroot or tapioca flour
80 g (2¾ oz) nut butter or seed butter
pinch sea salt flakes
120 g (4½ oz) raw or dark chocolate (at least 70% cocoa solids), chopped
60 g (2 oz/½ cup) hemp seeds

Preheat the oven to 180°C (350°F) and line a 20 x 15 cm (8 x 6 in) baking tin with baking paper.

Place the linseed meal and 125 ml (4 fl oz/½ cup) water in a large mixing bowl and stand for a few minutes, or until the water has been absorbed.

Add the baking powder, bicarbonate of soda, raw cacao powder, maple syrup, coconut nectar, vanilla and arrowroot flour and mix until well combined.

Add the nut butter and stir until the mixture is smooth then add the salt, chocolate and hemp seeds.

Pour into the tin and bake for 25 minutes or until just set.

Cool the brownie in the tin for at least 15 minutes (if you can wait that long) before slicing into 12 even-sized pieces.

NOTE
Hemp seeds can be left out of this recipe and replaced with a nut or another type of seed, such as crushed walnuts or pepitas (pumpkin seeds). Alternatively, they can be substituted with additional chocolate for a complete chocolate overload... or with nothing at all!

DOUGHNUTS

MAKES 12
Preparation time: 15 minutes
Cooking time: 25 minutes

I love doughnuts; cinnamon sugar doughnuts, iced doughnuts, jam doughnuts, Nutella doughnuts, doughnut bites – literally all doughnuts! But I just happen to be coeliac and refined sugars make me feel gross. So if I do want a doughnut, I have to make one myself. These doughnuts are grain-free, gluten-free, vegan, dairy-free and refined sugar-free but... they are also AWESOME! They look like real doughnuts, taste like doughnuts and, to me, that's a win-win-win.

400 g (14 oz) tin chickpeas, chilled
100 g (3½ oz/⅔ cup) linseed
　(flax seed) meal
200 g (7 oz/2 cups) ground almonds
80 g (2¾ oz) arrowroot or tapioca flour
50 g (1¾ oz) coconut flour
100 g (3½ oz) coconut sugar
1½ teaspoons baking powder
½ teaspoon bicarbonate of soda
　(baking soda)

250 ml (9 fl oz/1 cup) almond milk
60 ml (2 fl oz/¼ cup) coconut oil
1 teaspoon vanilla extract or
　½ teaspoon vanilla powder

TOPPINGS

150 g (5½ oz) raw, dark or caramel milk
　chocolate, melted and cooled
bee pollen, coconut 'bacon' (see
　page 134), activated buckwheat
　(see page 11), coconut flakes or
　cacao nibs, for sprinkling

Preheat the oven to 180°C (350°F).

Drain the chickpeas well, reserving the liquid. Place the liquid in the bowl of an electric mixer. Using the whisk attachment, whisk it on high speed until it's very thick and fluffy, like meringue. Set aside.

Stir the linseed meal and 60 ml (2 fl oz/¼ cup) water together in a bowl.

Place the ground almonds, arrowroot flour, coconut flour, coconut sugar, baking powder and bicarbonate of soda in a mixing bowl. Add the almond milk, coconut oil, vanilla and linseed meal mixture and stir until combined.

Gently fold in the whisked chickpea liquid using a large metal spoon, taking care not to deflate it too much as this will affect the lightness of your doughnuts.

Distribute the mixture evenly among 12 non-stick standard doughnut-shaped moulds. Bake for 20–25 minutes, or until cooked through and golden.

Remove from the oven and allow to cool completely.

Once completely cooled, dip one side of each doughnut into melted chocolate, letting any excess drain off, then sprinkle with your preferred toppings.

Enjoy immediately, or store in an airtight container in the fridge. Doughnuts will keep for a couple of days.

CHOCOLATE CHUNK COOKIES

MAKES 22
Preparation time: 15 minutes, plus 30 minutes chilling
Cooking time: 15 minutes

The chocolate chip cookie really is the king of the cookie world, and this version is vegan, gluten-free, paleo, refined sugar-free and egg-free. And it can be made nut-free too, if you want! That in no way means these are fun-free though, as they're as fun and tasty as can be! They're perfect with a morning or afternoon cuppa, or just for sneaking in throughout the day as a little snack.

100 g (3½ oz/1 cup) ground almonds (or sunflower seeds ground to a fine meal)

30 g (1 oz/¼ cup) arrowroot or tapioca flour

2½ tablespoons coconut flour

1 teaspoon bicarbonate of soda (baking soda)

60 ml (2 fl oz/¼ cup) coconut oil, slightly softened

¼ teaspoon vanilla powder

90 g (3 oz/⅓ cup) nut or seed butter

75 g (2¾ oz/½ cup) coconut sugar

2½ tablespoons maple syrup

120 g (4½ oz) raw or dark chocolate (at least 70% cocoa solids), roughly chopped

pinch sea salt flakes

2 tablespoons white chia seeds or linseed (flax seed) meal

Preheat the oven to 180°C (350°F) and line a baking tray with baking paper.

Combine all the ingredients in a mixing bowl with 60 ml (2 fl oz/¼ cup) water and stir together to form a dough. Or you can use an electric mixer, fitted with the paddle attachment, to mix if you prefer.

Wrap the dough in plastic wrap then refrigerate for at least 30 minutes to firm up a bit. (I know, it's hard – I don't want to wait either but you have to trust me when I say chilling the dough makes for a better cookie!)

Remove the dough from the fridge then roll into 3.5 cm (1½ in) balls and place on the baking tray. Gently flatten them with the back of a fork then bake for 12–15 minutes or until golden.

Allow to cool before nibbling. Store in an airtight container, at room temperature, for up to 1 week.

BEET, BERRY & CHOCOLATE MUFFINS

MAKES 12
Preparation time: 15 minutes
Cooking time: 20–25 minutes

I am going to be the worst mum, and by that I really mean I am going to be the best mum because I am SO good at sneaking vegetables into everything. These muffins are one of the best chocolate muffins ever. You would never even know there is beetroot in them and they taste just amazing. These can also be made nut-free by substituting the ground almonds for sunflower seed meal, or any other gluten-free flour alternative.

2½ tablespoons linseed (flax seed) meal
90 g (3 oz/¾ cup) raw cacao powder
2 teaspoons baking powder
1 teaspoon bicarbonate of soda (baking soda)
130 g (4½ oz/1 cup) buckwheat flour
100 g (3½ oz/1 cup) ground almonds
30 g (1 oz/¼ cup) arrowroot or tapioca flour
225 g (8 oz/1½ cups) coconut sugar, or 250 ml (8½ fl oz/1 cup) maple syrup

100 g (3½ oz) dark chocolate (at least 70% cocoa solids), chopped
160 ml (5½ fl oz/⅔ cup) coconut oil
250 ml (8½ fl oz/1 cup) coconut cream
1 medium beetroot (beet) (about 150g/ 5½ oz), peeled and grated
pinch sea salt flakes
150 g (5½ oz) mixed frozen berries

Preheat the oven to 180°C (350°F).

Combine the linseed meal and 120 ml (4 fl oz) water in a large bowl and stand for a few minutes, until the water has been absorbed.

Add the raw cacao powder, baking powder, bicarbonate of soda, buckwheat flour, ground almonds, arrowroot, coconut sugar and dark chocolate and stir to combine well. Stir in the coconut oil, coconut cream, grated beetroot and salt until combined then add the berries.

Line a 12-hole muffin tin with paper muffin cases, then divide the mixture evenly between them. Transfer to the oven and bake for 20–25 minutes or until the tops have cracked and the muffins are cooked through.

Allow to cool in the tins before serving.

NOTE

Due to the lack of refined sugars in here and the presence of berries and beetroot, these only last for 3–4 days, in an airtight container at room temperature. But they'll keep longer in the fridge. If you refrigerate them though, you may just want to warm them slightly before serving.

QUINOA, BUCKWHEAT & TAHINI LUNCHBOX BARS

MAKES 14
Preparation time: 15 minutes
Setting time: about 2½ hours

I don't have much to say about these, except that they are totally nut-free and totally awesome. They're the perfect lunchbox bar or snack bar to have whenever you want a bit of pop and crunch in your mouth!

12 medjool dates (about 240 g/8½ oz), pitted
60 g (2 oz/½ cup) hemp seeds or sesame seeds
180 g (6½ oz/⅔ cup) tahini
2½ tablespoons coconut oil
2 tablespoons raw honey or rice malt syrup
pinch sea salt flakes
50 g (1¾ oz/1 cup) puffed quinoa

90 g (3 oz/⅔ cup) pepitas (pumpkin seeds)
60 g (2 oz/⅓ cup) activated buckwheat (see page 11)
40 g (1½ oz/⅓ cup) sunflower seeds

TOPPING
80 g (2¾ oz) raw chocolate, melted and cooled
hemp seeds or desiccated coconut, for sprinkling, optional

Place the dates, hemp seeds, tahini, coconut oil, honey and salt in your food processor or blender and process until smooth.

Transfer to a mixing bowl and add the puffed quinoa, pepitas, activated buckwheat and sunflower seeds. You may need to get your hands in there to properly mix this one; just make sure you've washed those grubby mitts beforehand!

Line the base of a 20 x 15 cm (8 x 6 in) baking tin with baking paper. Transfer the mixture to the tin, pressing it firmly and evenly over the base, then refrigerate for about 2½ hours, or until firm. Pour over the melted chocolate and return to the fridge to set.

Cut into 14 even-sized squares and transfer them to an airtight container in the fridge or freezer. These will keep for up to 2 weeks in the fridge, and a couple of months in the freezer.

NOTE
For these bars to become super firm, substitute the coconut oil with 40 g (1½ oz) cacao butter (melted).

BREAKFAST BARS

MAKES 10–12 BARS
Preparation time: 10 minutes
Setting time: about 2½ hours

This recipe is inspired by the breakfast bar my friend Ryo makes at my favourite Melbourne eatery, Walk Don't Run, and they're as mindful and as goodness-packed as they come. They're super delicious, foolproof to whip up and make a winning breakfast when you're running out of time. (Or sprinting out the door.) I can also endorse these bars as wonderful hiking snacks.

185 g (6½ oz/1½ cups) sunflower seeds

105 g (3½ oz/¾ cup) pepitas (pumpkin seeds)

50 g (1¾ oz/¼ cup) goji berries

40 g (1½ oz/¼ cup) sesame seeds

40 g (1½ oz/¼ cup) cacao nibs (optional; these can be substituted with another seed or nut)

40 g (1½ oz/¼ cup) white chia seeds

45 g (1½ oz/¼ cup) linseeds (flax seeds)

175 g (6 oz/½ cup) raw honey or rice malt syrup

90 g (3 oz/⅓ cup) tahini, cashew butter or other seed butter

40 g (1½ oz) cacao butter, melted

Place all the ingredients in a bowl and mix with a wooden spoon until well combined.

Line the base of a 20 x 15 cm (8 x 6 in) baking tin with baking paper. Transfer the mixture to the tin, pressing it firmly and evenly over the base then refrigerate for 2½ hours or until firm.

Once the mixture is firm, cut into 10–12 even-sized bars. Store in an airtight container in the fridge for up to 2 weeks, or in the freezer for up to 2 months.

RAW LEMON SLICE

MAKES 12
Preparation time: 15 minutes
Setting time: 1–2 hours

Lemon slice was always my faaaaaaaaavourite when I was little. The sweet–sour flavour of lemon combined with coconut is just one of the best things to eat, ever. This is a delicious raw version of the classic lemon slice, and it's as easy to make as it is to eat!

BASE
155 g (5½ oz/1 cup) activated raw cashews or macadamia nuts (see page 11)

45 g (1½ oz/½ cup) desiccated coconut

2½ tablespoons ground almonds

½ teaspoon vanilla extract or ¼ teaspoon vanilla powder

2 tablespoons maple syrup, coconut nectar or rice malt syrup

finely grated zest of 1 lemon

ICING
155 g (5½ oz/1 cup) activated raw cashews (see page 11)

2½ tablespoons coconut butter or coconut paste

½ teaspoon vanilla extract

finely grated zest of 1 lemon

60 ml (2 fl oz/¼ cup) lemon juice

2½ tablespoons coconut cream

2½ tablespoons coconut nectar

For the base, place all the ingredients into your food processor or blender then pulse together until combined.

Line the base of a 20 x 15 cm (8 x 6 in) baking tin with baking paper. Transfer the mixture to the tin, pressing it firmly and evenly over the base, then freeze it for 30–60 minutes to firm.

To make the icing, combine all the ingredients in the cleaned food processor and process until smooth. Remove the slice from the freezer and pour the icing over the base. Spread it so it covers evenly then return to the freezer for about 30–60 minutes to set.

Once set, cut into 12 even-sized bars and store in an airtight container in the fridge or freezer. They'll keep for a few days in the fridge, and up to 1 month in the freezer.

BANOFFEE 'NICE' CREAM SUNDAE

SERVES 2–4
Preparation time: 20 minutes

Banoffee pie is just so inviting – it's food porn at it's best. Oozy caramel, soft banana and crunchy bits on top. Mmmmmmmm. This sundae is a combination of all of those things and as soon as it's made, you'll totally want to smash your face into it. But I know you'll restrain yourself and stay classy.

'NICE' CREAM

4 small frozen peeled bananas (about 440 g/15½ oz)

125 ml (4 fl oz/½ cup) coconut cream, chilled

2 medjool dates (about 40 g/1½ oz), pitted

1 teaspoon vanilla extract or ½ teaspoon vanilla powder

2½ tablespoons maple syrup

PEANUT CARAMEL SAUCE

3 medjool dates (about 60 g/2 oz), pitted

125 g (4½ oz) nut or seed butter

80 ml (2½ fl oz/⅓ cup) coconut cream

2½ tablespoons coconut oil

pinch sea salt flakes

60 ml (2 fl oz/¼ cup) maple syrup

1 teaspoon vanilla extract

TOPPINGS

chopped bliss balls, chopped chocolate, activated buckwheat (see page 11) or coconut 'bacon' (see page 134), to taste

Place all the 'nice' cream ingredients into your food processor or blender. Process them until they're completely smooth. Scoop the mixture into a container or bowl and place it in the freezer until it's firm.

To make the peanut caramel sauce, place all the ingredients into the cleaned food processor or blender and process until smooth.

To assemble, layer scoops of the 'nice' cream and caramel sauce in chilled bowls or glasses. Sprinkle with the toppings of your choice and serve immediately. Everyone will love you.

BERRY RED SUPERPOPS

MAKES 10
Preparation time: 5 minutes
Setting time: 4 hours

Berries are delicious and this recipe is packed with so many antioxidants and goodies, they will keep you feeling beautiful and young. These are also a perfect way to sneak nutrient-rich goodies into your kids. With their bright colour and great taste (just like a really good icy pole), children will hoover these up.

225 g (8 oz/1½ cups) mixed frozen berries

2½ tablespoons acai powder

4 small bananas (about 440 g/15½ oz), peeled

1 small beetroot (beet) (about 80 g/2¾ oz), peeled and chopped

2½ tablespoons raw honey or maple syrup

2 teaspoons vanilla extract or 1 teaspoon vanilla powder

juice of 1 lemon

Place all the ingredients in your food processor or blender and blend until smooth. Spoon the mixture into six 85 ml (2¾ fl oz) popsicle moulds and place them in the freezer for a couple of hours or until partially frozen. Push a popsicle stick halfway into each one, down the middle, and freeze for another 2 or so hours, or until they are frozen hard. To serve, dip the moulds briefly in hot water to loosen then carefully pull each one out.

NOTE
Throw in some optional extras – chia seeds, goji berries and cacao nibs, for example – as you see fit.

(pictured on page 118)

CHOCO SUPERPOPS

MAKES 6
Preparation time: 5 minutes
Setting time: 4 hours

Some days you really just want a chocolate ice cream and for those occasions, these really are the bomb diggity! They're the absolute perfect combo of smoothie and ice cream – you really can't go wrong!

2 bananas (about 220 g/8 oz), peeled
¼ ripe avocado
125 ml (4 fl oz/½ cup) almond milk
1 tablespoon cashew or seed butter

2 medjool dates (about 40 g/1½ oz), pitted
2 tablespoons raw cacao powder
1 teaspoon vanilla extract or ½ teaspoon vanilla powder
½ teaspoon ground cinnamon

Place all the ingredients in your food processor or blender and blend until smooth. Spoon the mixture into six 85 ml (2¾ fl oz) popsicle moulds and place in the freezer for a couple of hours or until partially frozen. Push a popsicle stick halfway into each one, down the middle, and freeze for another 2 or so hours or until they are frozen hard. To serve, dip the moulds briefly in hot water to loosen then carefully pull each one out.

NOTE
Throw in some optional extras – chia seeds, goji berries and cacao nibs, for example – as you see fit.

(pictured on page 119)

Nº 5

DRINKS

CHIA LEMONADE

SERVES 2–4
Preparation time: 5 minutes

This drink is what I reach for when I get home from work, or whenever anyone comes over for dinner. It's quick to make, refreshing, and it also looks super pretty on the table. This is also an excellent drink for bottling and taking with you to work, or to use as a liquid pick-me-up when you're out. Just make sure you use white chia seeds as the black ones look like you've got ants in your drink. Which isn't terribly glamorous.

2 tablespoons lemon juice
zest of 1 lemon
½ lemon, thinly sliced
2 tablespoons maple syrup

750 ml (25½ fl oz/3 cups) sparkling water, chilled
5 mint sprigs
1 tablespoon white chia seeds
205 g (7 oz/1½ cups) ice cubes

Place all the ingredients in a large pitcher and stir together. Stand the mixture for a few minutes to allow the chia seeds to swell, then stir again just before serving.

CARAMEL, BANANA & MACA 'MILKSHAKE'

Somewhere in between Smoothie Land and Milkshake-ville comes this – my version of a milkshake! It's a total treat for those times when you want something naughty. Add some frozen avocado chunks or ice cubes, for an even frothier shake.

1 large frozen peeled banana (about 150 g/5½ oz)

2 teaspoons maca powder

1½ teaspoons mesquite powder

3 medjool dates (about 60 g/2 oz), pitted

½ teaspoon vanilla extract or ¼ teaspoon vanilla powder

3 teaspoons cashew butter or seed butter

500 ml (17 fl oz/2 cups) almond milk, chilled

optional extras – chia seeds, bee pollen, linseed (flax seed) meal

Place all the ingredients in your blender and blend until smooth and frothy. Pour into 2–4 glasses and serve immediately.

NOTE
To make this into a 'thick shake' add a scoop of 'nice' cream (see page 114) coconut milk ice cream or nut milk ice cream (refined sugar-free, of course!).

STRAWBERRY & GOJI 'MILKSHAKE'

This is a grown-ups version of a strawberry milkshake, for times when you realise you're too old for a milkshake but really, really want one (we've all been there). Add some frozen avocado chunks or ice cubes, for an even frothier shake.

300 g (10½ oz/2 cups) frozen strawberries

2½ tablespoons goji berries

½ teaspoon vanilla extract or ¼ teaspoon vanilla powder

1 tablespoon cashew butter

1 tablespoon raw honey or coconut nectar

500 ml (17 fl oz/2 cups) almond milk, chilled

optional extras – camu camu powder, berry flavoured plant-based protein powder, chia seeds, cacao nibs

Place all the ingredients into your blender and blend until smooth. Pour into 2–4 glasses and serve immediately.

SUPERSTARTER COFFEE

SERVES 2
Preparation time: 3 minutes

I luuuuuurve me some coffee and boy does this provide a good start to your day! This coffee really does give an extra energy kick, whilst keeping any acidity at bay with the addition of cardamom. It's the perfect morning beverage to get you through to lunch, and a great accompaniment to a bliss ball or two! If you're a milky coffee person, just add some frothed-up coconut or almond milk and sprinkle with some additional ground cinnamon or raw cacao powder – delicious!

500 ml (17 fl oz/2 cups) freshly
   brewed coffee
1 teaspoon cacao powder
½ teaspoon ground cinnamon
pinch ground cardamom

pinch cayenne pepper
pinch pink sea salt flakes
1–2 teaspoons maple syrup, to taste
1 teaspoon coconut oil
1 teaspoon reishi powder (optional)

Combine all the ingredients in a small saucepan and place over low heat. Using a wooden spoon, stir to combine well until everything is hot – about 3 minutes. Pour into two glasses and enjoy.

MOCHA ENERGY SMOOTHIE

SERVES 2
Preparation time: 5 minutes

Packed with protein and energising ingredients, this smoothie will wake you up and keep you fuelled! This is one of my favourite smoothies to make when I've slept in and am running late, as it knocks together two cravings in one – coffee and smoothie. Ah-mazing! Insanely creamy, with the addition of avocado and frozen banana; it's the perfect morning drink for when you just have to get up and GO!

1 large frozen peeled banana (about 150 g/5½ oz)

¼ avocado, flesh only (about 40 g/1½ oz)

125 ml (4 fl oz/½ cup) cold brewed coffee or chilled espresso

375 ml (12½ fl oz/1½ cups) almond milk, chilled

2½ tablespoons ABC (almond, brazil and cashew butter), or nut or seed butter

1 tablespoon tahini

2 medjool dates (about 40 g/1½ oz), pitted

2 tablespoons cacao powder

1 tablespoon maple syrup (optional)

½ teaspoon cordyceps or reishi powder (optional)

Place all the ingredients into your blender and blend until smooth. Pour into two glasses and enjoy immediately.

TROPICAL GREEN SMOOTHIE

SERVES 2
Preparation time: 5 minutes

Often when I make a smoothie, I make enough for 2 or 3 serves at a time. I will then pour myself a glass and bottle the rest to take to work, or just put it in the fridge for those moments when I CBB (can't be bothered) making something healthy, but totally know I should. This smoothie is super-hydrating and, with the pineapple, really good for your gut – just make sure you keep the core in there to get the full benefit. It goes perfectly with Berry red superpops (see page 116), or a Fruit salad bliss bite (see page 32).

370 g (13 oz/2⅓ cups) chopped pineapple flesh, including the core
2 kale leaves
2½ tablespoons mint leaves, roughly chopped
juice of 1 lemon, or to taste
125 ml (4 fl oz/½ cup) coconut water
1 tablespoon raw honey or maple syrup
½ teaspoon matcha powder (optional)
2 teaspoons lucuma powder (optional)

Place all the ingredients into your blender and blend until smooth. Pour into two glasses and enjoy immediately.

NOTE
Add ice, or use frozen pineapple, for a thicker smoothie. If using frozen pineapple, add a bit more coconut water, as required, for blending.

GOLDEN MILK

SERVES 2
Preparation time: 5 minutes

'Golden milk' is a great way to end your day, and the perfect after-dinner beverage.
I find hot chocolate contains too much caffeine for a lot of people to enjoy at night,
so this drink is an excellent alternative. Loaded with beneficial spices, it goes beyond
just being warming and comforting. Use any plant-based milk you prefer here.

500 ml (17 fl oz/2 cups) almond,
  coconut or hemp milk
1½ teaspoons ground turmeric
1 teaspoon ground cinnamon
pinch ground cardamom
pinch ground ginger
pinch freshly ground black pepper

pinch freshly grated nutmeg
1 teaspoon bee pollen (optional)
½ teaspoon vanilla extract or
  ¼ teaspoon vanilla powder
2 tablespoons raw honey, maple syrup
  or coconut nectar
pinch ground chilli (if you like it spicy!)

Place all the ingredients in a small saucepan and bring to a simmer over low heat,
stirring every so often. Once warmed to your liking, pour into two cups and serve.

Nº 6

BASICS & ACCOMPANIMENTS

COCONUT 'BACON'

MAKES 65 G (2¼ OZ/1 CUP)
Preparation time: 5 minutes
Cooking time: 5 minutes

This is maybe the easiest and the best thing you will make from this book.
Use it for topping your truffles, sprinkling on salads or for coating cashew cheese balls
(see page 59). There is nothing that these bacon pieces don't go with!

55 g (2 oz/1 cup) coconut flakes
1 teaspoon maple syrup
1 teaspoon tamari
1 teaspoon coconut oil

½ teaspoon smoked paprika
pinch sea salt flakes
1–2 drops liquid smoke (optional)

Preheat the oven to 180°C (350°F) and line a baking tray with baking paper.

Place all the ingredients in a mixing bowl and stir together so the coconut is coated in everything.

Spread the coconut mixture on the lined baking tray and bake for around 5 minutes or until golden. Let it cool completely then transfer it to an airtight jar and store at room temperature. It will keep for 1 month.

RAW CHOCOLATE

MAKES 350 G (12½ OZ/1 CUP)
Preparation time: 10 minutes
Setting time: 20 minutes

Raw chocolate is one of those things that can be madly expensive to buy, and is really quite easy to make at home. This is a very simple recipe and you can use it for any other recipe in this book that uses chocolate – or just eat it whenever you feel the need (no judgement here). You can substitute the cacao butter with coconut oil, but as soon as you pull the chocolate out of the fridge it will start to soften and it doesn't really hold its shape as well when used in baking. So really, what I'm saying is, stick to the cacao butter.

175 g (6 oz) cacao butter
90 g (3 oz/¼ cup) agave syrup
  or maple syrup
85 g (3 oz/⅔ cup) raw cacao powder
pinch sea salt flakes, plus extra for
  sprinkling

2½ tablespoons coconut cream (optional)
toppings of your choice: extra sea salt
  flakes, chopped nuts, chopped dried
  fruits, or seeds

Melt the cacao butter in a double boiler set over simmering water. Once it's melted, whisk in the agave syrup then add the cacao, salt and coconut cream (if using). Whisk again until the mixture is smooth then remove from the heat and cool slightly. Line the base of a 20 x 15 cm (8 x 6 in) tray with baking paper. Pour in the chocolate mixture then sprinkle with a little extra salt, or other topping of your choice.

Place in the fridge or freezer for about 20 minutes to set then chop up and enjoy.

RAW CHOCOLATE BITES

MAKES ABOUT 24
Preparation time: 5 minutes
Setting time: 20 minutes

These are super-quick, easy-to-make little chocolate bites, which are great to have in
the freezer. Then, when you need a little somethin' (in case all the balls you already have
in your fridge/freezer aren't enough), you can grab a square or two
and eat at your leisure.

175 g (6 oz) cacao butter
60 ml (2 fl oz/¼ cup) agave syrup
   or maple syrup
85 g (3 oz/⅔ cup) raw cacao powder
pinch sea salt flakes, plus extra for topping
   (optional)

2½ tablespoons coconut cream (optional)
toppings of your choice: chopped nuts,
   chopped dried fruits, coconut flakes
   seeds

Melt the cacao butter in a double boiler set over simmering water. Once it's melted,
whisk in the agave syrup then add the cacao, salt and coconut cream (if using). Whisk
again until the mixture is smooth then remove from the heat and cool slightly. Line
the base of a 20 x 15 cm (8 x 6 in) tray with baking paper. Pour in the chocolate
mixture then sprinkle with a little extra salt, or other topping of your choice.

Place in the fridge or freezer to set completely. Chop and enjoy.

SALTED CARAMEL SPREAD

MAKES 350 G (12½ OZ/1 CUP)
Preparation time: 5 minutes

This spread is like *daayum*, as they say on the street. So easy to make, so perfect to spread on everything in sight and just really, really tasty. Use it as a filling for truffles, spread it on toast with banana or just eat it by the spoonful.

12 medjool dates (about 240 g/8½ oz), pitted
125 g (4½ oz) nut butter or tahini

2½ tablespoons maple syrup
pinch sea salt flakes
2½ tablespoons coconut paste (optional)

Place all the ingredients in your food processor or blender and process until smooth. Transfer to a sterilised jar (see page 11) and store in the fridge, where it will keep for 2 weeks.

VEGAN PEANUT BUTTER
DOG BISCUITS

MAKES 24 BISCUITS
Preparation time: 30 minutes
Cooking time: 15 minutes

I couldn't create a book of treats for humans without creating at least one for my furry friends. I always want to treat my puppies to something nice (as pet owners do), however I can't always afford the fancy treats found at the farmers' markets. So I decided to create my own, with the help of my mum, and with the taste testing by my dogs. These treats are super easy to make and they got the lick of approval by all three of my puppies. All the ingredients are also considered safe for doggos, however it's always a good idea to check your pooch has no hidden allergies or sensitivities before giving them a whole treat.

100 g (3½ oz) sweet potato, peeled and roughly chopped
100 g (3½ oz) carrot, roughly chopped
110 g (4 oz/1 cup) besan (chickpea flour)

60 g (2 oz/¼ cup) sugar- and xylitol-free peanut butter
15 g (½ oz/¼ cup) quinoa puffs or flakes
doggy carob chips and linseed (flax seed) meal (optional)

Preheat the oven to 180°C (350°F).

Steam the sweet potato and carrot in a double boiler set over medium heat for about 12 minutes, or until just soft. Mash until smooth.

Add the remaining ingredients and mix well. The mixture will be stiff and slightly sticky due to the peanut butter.

Lightly dust a work surface with chickpea flour. Roll out the dough to 3 mm (⅛ in) thick. Cut into 5 x 4 cm (2 x 1½ in) pieces and shape into dog bones using your hands. Alternatively, use a dog bone-shaped cookie cutter of around the same size.

Place on a tray lined with baking paper and bake for 10 minutes. Flip and bake for a further 5 minutes, or until golden.

Transfer to a wire rack to cool completely.

Store in an airtight container for 1–2 weeks.

ABOUT KATE BRADLEY

Australian-born, 26 year old Kate Bradley is a plant-based cook, food stylist and recipe developer based in Melbourne, Australia. Kate first gave up refined sugar, gluten and all processed foods in late 2012, which completely revolutionised her health and wellbeing, not to mention her cooking style.

Kate is as passionate about health as she is about cooking and eating. Kate discovered her love of cooking at a young age and quickly evolved a plant-based approach to cooking that focuses on delicious, nourishing whole foods and recipes that are simple enough to cook every day. Kate started the Kenkō Kitchen website to share her passion for simple, tasty and healthy whole foods with the rest of the world and to inspire other young cooks.

Since beginning Kenkō Kitchen, Kate has been dedicated to making plant-based eating easy, delicious and achievable in people's everyday, busy lives.

When Kate is not in the kitchen recipe developing, she is working on her Melbourne based coffee business, Rushmore Coffee, or hanging out with her dogs (and part-time kitchen hands) Reggie, Waz & Peanut.

THANK YOU

When I got the opportunity to write my first cookbook, I was overwhelmed. It had been my dream since I first picked up a wooden spoon to help my nanna (Shirley) bake when I was a child. There is nothing else more calming and more fulfilling than making people smile through my food. Having the support to now create a second book has just been incredible, and again, something I could have only dreamed about.

To my mum Roni, thank you for being the best mother (and friend) in the world. Thank you for always being my biggest support. Thank you for still being there to hug me and wipe my tears when I'm stressed, even though I'm 26 years old. Thank you for always inspiring me with your cool ideas and recipe concepts. Thank you for always recipe testing everything for me when I am short on time. Thank you for buying ingredients, weighing things, rolling things and checking things. You work so hard without expecting anything in return. I wouldn't be able to achieve all that I do and I couldn't have got this book done without you!

To Elisa, thank you for everything you have done for me being the second-half of Kenkō. You believed in me from the beginning, and have always been there to encourage me and help me grow. There would be no Kenkō without you! You're so talented and amazing, and you constantly motivate and inspire me!

To my partner, Bulut, thank you for eating 4,000 bliss balls. Even when they probably should have been thrown out, you still dumpstered them down, wasting nothing. Thank you for all your support while I was stressed and for always knowing how to calm me down (food, puppies, Netflix). You always inspire me to keep going and I'm very grateful to have you as my best friend and boyfriend. Thanks for pushing me when I need it.

Thank you to Sally, dad and Tim. I feel like you are always helping me with everything. What would I do without all your sage advise in the family Whatsapp group? I'd be a mess! I'm lucky to have such talented and supportive older siblings and a great dad who always wants to push me further and in the right direction. You guys are so smart and I love you.

To Dustin, I thank you for being my most patient best friend and business partner. You are always there for me and I am forever grateful I have you in my life. Thank you for looking after Rushmore with Bulut while I wrote this book and for always inspiring me with your insane food and life talents. I'm still certain you're not actually human and must be an alien.

A massive thank you to Carrie and Claire for seriously being my two biggest cheerleaders and for also eating copius amounts of balls. Thank you for always giving me your honest feedback. Thank you for testing for me and for just being amazing with me even when all I could do is stress-dance in front of you. You two were there for me during my numerous mini breakdowns and were huge supports for me. I love you two so freakin' much! Thank you to also selling my books to strangers in department stores, and for always embarrassing me in the best ways.

Thank you to Ella, Chloe, Ross, Nick and Emily for being awesome friends. For trialling balls, eating balls and just for all your support in general! You guys rule.

Thank you to Jane Willson and my awesome team at Hardie Grant! I am soooo lucky I have you guys. Thank you for giving me the chance to make a second book and for believing in me (and all my visions)!

Thank you to Andrea for being so, so patient with me and for being the best support. Thanks for all you do behind the scenes and all that you have done to get this book finished. Thanks for pushing me and for supporting me and for loving my slice.

Thank you to Emily for your design skills, Leanne for your editing skills (my nonsense sure needed it!) and to the rest of the team who have been there working away behind the scenes.

I'd also like to thank you, Caroline, for your beautiful styling, for lending your studio and 'getting' my vision, and to Lindsay for being the best help ever during the shoot. Dream team.

Thank you as well to Reggie, Waz and Peanut for being super cute dogs and for always making me smile every time I walk through the door.

Cue Academy Award get-off-stage music.

Published in 2017 by Hardie Grant Books,
an imprint of Hardie Grant Publishing

Hardie Grant Books (Melbourne)
Building 1, 658 Church Street
Richmond, Victoria 3121

Hardie Grant Books (London)
5th & 6th Floors
52–54 Southwark Street
London SE1 1UN

hardiegrantbooks.com

A Cataloguing-in-Publication entry is available from
the catalogue of the National Library of Australia at
www.nla.gov.au

Bliss Bites
ISBN 978 1 74379 357 2

Publishing Director: Jane Willson
Managing Editor: Marg Bowman
Project Editor: Andrea O'Connor
Editor: Leanne Kitchen
Design Manager: Jessica Lowe
Designer: Emily O'Neill
Photographer: Elisa Watson
Stylist: Caroline Velik
Home Economist: Lindsay Harris
Production Manager: Todd Rechner
Production Coordinator: Tessa Spring

Colour reproduction by Splitting Image Colour Studio
Printed in China by Leo Paper Products Ltd.